SCHOPENHAUER, WOMEN'S LITERATURE, AND
THE LEGACY OF PESSIMISM IN THE NOVELS OF
GEORGE ELIOT, OLIVE SCHREINER,
VIRGINIA WOOLF, AND DORIS LESSING

SCHOPENHAUER, WOMEN'S LITERATURE, AND THE LEGACY OF PESSIMISM IN THE NOVELS OF GEORGE ELIOT, OLIVE SCHREINER, VIRGINIA WOOLF, AND DORIS LESSING

Penelope LeFew-Blake

Studies in Comparative Literature
Volume 42

The Edwin Mellen Press
Lewiston•Queenston•Lampeter

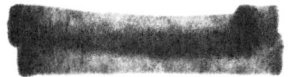

Library of Congress Cataloging-in-Publication Data

LeFew-Blake, Penelope.
　Schopenhauer, women's literature, and the legacy of pessimism in the novels of George Eliot, Olive Schreiner, Virginia Woolf, and Doris Lessing / Penelope LeFew-Blake.
　　　p. cm. -- (Studies in comparative literature ; v. 42)
　Includes bibliographical references and index.
　ISBN 0-7734-7437-4
　1. English fiction--Women authors--History and criticism. 2. Pessimism in literature. 3. Women and literature--Great Britain--History--20th century. 4. Women and literature--Great Britain--History--19th century. 5. Schopenhauer, Arthur, 1788-1860--Influence. 6. Schreiner, Olive, 1855-1920--Philosophy. 7. Woolf, Virginia, 1882-1941--Philosophy. 8. Lessing, Doris May, 1919--Philosophy. 9. Eliot, George, 1819-1880--Philosophy. 10. English fiction--German influences. I. Title. II. Studies in comparative literature (Lewiston, N.Y.) ; v. 42.

PR888.P444 L44　2001
823'.809353--dc21

2001030288

```
This is volume 42 in the continuing series
Studies in Comparative Literature
Volume 42 ISBN 0-7734-7437-4
SCL Series ISBN 0-88946-393-X
```

A CIP catalog record for this book is available from the British Library.

Copyright　©　2001　Penelope LeFew-Blake

Front Cover: Valentine Cameron Prinsep (1838-1904)
　　　　Study of a Girl Reading (c. 1860s-70s)

All rights reserved. For information contact

　　　　The Edwin Mellen Press　　　　　　The Edwin Mellen Press
　　　　　　　Box 450　　　　　　　　　　　　　　Box 67
　　　　Lewiston, New York　　　　　　　Queenston, Ontario
　　　　USA 14092-0450　　　　　　　　　CANADA L0S 1L0

　　　　　　　The Edwin Mellen Press, Ltd.
　　　　　　　Lampeter, Ceredigion, Wales
　　　　　　　UNITED KINGDOM SA48 8LT

Printed in the United States of America

Dedication

This book is dedicated to my mother, Carrie Jones LeFew; my father, William Rosser LeFew; my husband, Hugh Kenneth Blake; and my dearest friend, Candice Haffner Joern. All of you have made Schopenhauer's philosophy a theory rather than a reality in my life.

Table of Contents

Preface		i
Introduction		1
Chapter One		
	Part One: George Eliot's *Middlemarch*: A Schopenhauerian Shadowplay	13
	Part Two: George Eliot's *Daniel Deronda*: A Study in Schopenhauerian Morality	35
Chapter Two	"A Striving and a Striving": Schopenhauerian Pessimism in Olive Schreiner's *The Story of an African Farm* and *From Man to Man*	49
Chapter Three	Virginia Woolf, Bloomsbury Aesthetics, And Schopenhauer	69
Chapter Four		
	Part One: Doris Lessing's *Children of Violence*: The Schopenhauerian Education of Martha Quest	89
	Part Two: Doris Lessing's *The Fifth Child*: The Will Personified	115
Conclusion		121
Notes		123
Bibliography		127
Index		133

Preface

This book attempts to counter a canonical line of thinking that presents Arthur Schopenhauer as an inveterate misogynist and, hence, of limited relevance to the wide, encompassing mélange that is women's studies. Actually, as the biographical record shows, misogynist or not, Schopenhauer was unflaggingly sensitive to the presence of women in his life. He worried incessantly about how they viewed him, and his inability to find a woman who would accept him caused him grave concern. Also, as this study makes clear, some very prominent women writers of both the nineteenth and twentieth centuries felt and acknowledged the influence of his philosophy of the "will" and reflect that influence in their works.

The degree to which Schopenhauer's influence shaped their thinking, however, requires a caution that Penelope LeFew Blake acknowledges in the introduction in her warning that Schopenhauer's influence in the waning years of the nineteenth century and the early years of the twentieth century tended to be felt as part of the afterglow of doctrines of pessimism and determinism that can be traced directly to Darwin and the 1850s. "Darwin," she writes, "gave scientific credence to the Schopenhauerian call for an acceptance of the world as it is" (13). Schopenhauer, consequently, was graced essentially with his "moment in time." As a harbinger of the changing conditions of the later nineteenth century (he died in 1860), he anticipates the philosophical milieu and, consequently, is the first great thinker to give serious expression to a cultural malaise that writers in particular associated with the *fin de siecle*. That writers should reflect Schopenhauer's philosophical influence comes as no surprise. He may have had more of a discernible impact on literature and contemporaneous literary figures than he did on the actual history of academic philosophy during his lifetime and well into the later years of the nineteenth century.

Literary influence studies, by their very nature, tend to be vulnerable to criticism on the basis often of their inability to measure exactly—citing chapter and verse—where influence is firmly documented. Of course, there are instances where the link between an author and an influence becomes common knowledge. In the case of Schopenhauer, in particular, the late nineteenth and early twentieth-century writer who comes immediately to mind as being most indebted to his thought is Thomas Mann. Yet even the influence of Schopenhauer on Mann, one that remains largely indisputable, is ambiguous and needs to be approached with considerable caution.

The precise influence Schopenhauer had on Mann probably will never be known for certain. When Mann, in the early years of his career, actually began seriously reading Schopenhauer remains problematic. In *Buddenbrooks*, published in 1901, Mann has Thomas Buddenbrooks read Schopenhauer in part ten, about three-fourths of the way through the book. The link to Schopenhauer here appears hard and concrete, but critics contend that Mann had not actually read into Schopenhauer in any depth until he began drafting the final chapters of the novel as late as 1899 or 1900. One could argue, therefore, along with T. J. Reed in *Thomas Mann: The Uses of Tradition* that the degree to which Schopenhauer influenced *Buddenbrooks*, Mann's first major success, is at best minimal (1996: 80-83). By 1914, when Mann begins writing *Reflections of a Nonpolitical Man*, the role played by Schopenhauer in the formation of his system of thought is far more clearly delineated. *Reflections*, published in 1918, almost twenty years after the inception of *Buddenbrooks*, is an introspective, self-analytical book that reveals the struggle that Mann was still undergoing as late in his career as 1918 to find an interconnectedness between his own strong convictions and the members of a distinct German philosophical tradition that at the time was in the ascendant. He could observe confidently in 1914 that, yes, he had actually drawn from Schopenhauer, Nietzsche and Wagner, "the triple constellation of eternally united spirits." Seeing himself then as the "reverent disciple" of each, he interprets their careers as representative of a culture and acknowledges how difficult it now is for him "to keep separate what he owes to each individually." He follows the acknowledgment of his indebtedness with the memorable admission, "I have Schopenhauer's morality—a popular word for the same thing is 'pessimism'—as my basic psychological mood" (1983:54).

Schopenhauer, Nietzsche and Wagner were central to a modern tradition of thought to which Mann by 1914 had openly attached himself. He acknowledges his deep connection to the spirit of the times, the nascence of twentieth-century "Modernism," which had been anticipated in earlier theories of decadence that had been current throughout Europe in the 1880s and 90s—the years of Mann's youth, of his literary apprenticeship, and of the genesis of *Buddenbrooks*. *Buddenbrooks* may not have been influenced directly by Schopenhauer in spite of Mann's decision to have Thomas Buddenbrooks read him, but the tenor of the novel treats in convincing detail the distinctly Schopenhauerian theme of the artistic will to create, though largely musical and Wagnerian in this case, as a defiant counter against an increasingly stultifying world of paralyzing respectability.

Penelope LeFew Blake has written a book that traces similar vestiges and echoes of Schopenhauer's influence through the lives and works of four prominent women authors—George Eliot, Olive Schreiner, Virginia Woolf and Doris Lessing. All four authors create characters who devour themselves in an effort to renew themselves. Though not solely artists, they reflect the struggles of Schopenhauer's artistic outsiders. Often, these struggles become an exercise in quiet desperation; at other times, they take the shape of a defiant, willful search for personal or artistic integrity. And although, like Mann's *Buddenbrooks*, concrete references to Schopenhauer in the fiction of these four women may be limited or non-existent, the world that informs their novels—a vision focused on the dilemmas and tragedies of real life in a real world dominated by suffering, struggle and disappointment—is, at its root, Schopenhauerian.

I am pleased to have had the opportunity to offer some contextual suggestions and some editorial assistance when this book was in its early drafts.

Franklin E. Court
Emeritus Professor of English
Northern Illinois University

Acknowledgments

I wish to express my gratitude to mentors who always demanded the best from me: Dr. Franklin Court, Northern Illinois University; the late Dr. J. Vail Foy, Carthage College; Mr. D. Loren Ingram; Dr. James I. Miller, Northern Illinois University; and Dr. Floyd C. Tolleson, Carthage College.

Introduction
Schopenhauer, Women, and Misogyny
I

Any thesis which suggests a sympathetic link between Arthur Schopenhauer and women is bound to raise a few eyebrows. Most people know him as a pessimist and a woman-hater. For some, like Virginia Woolf, these two characteristics were sufficient reason to hope to escape "for ever from the pages of Schopenhauer" (Woolf, *Essays* 157). Initially, then, the origins and impact of Schopenhauer's misogyny on his work must be examined before we can discuss those portions of Schopenhauer's philosophy which women writers have found so valuable.

Understandably, Schopenhauer formed his opinions about women on the basis of his life experiences. Schopenhauer's misogyny was not the result of warped insight into the nature of all women, and it was never actually an integral part of his philosophy. Rather, it was a personal, emotional reaction to a set of circumstances which he, regrettably, included in his two greatest philosophical works, *The World as Will and Representation* and *Parerga and Paralipomena*. Though his statements about women were the only sections of his philosophical works which he recanted at the end of his life, his reputation as a misogynist has provided feminist scholars their strongest justification to follow Woolf's lead and ignore Schopenhauer's relevance to women's studies.

Setting the record straight necessitates first reviewing the record. In *The*

World as Will and Representation, Schopenhauer stated, women "can have remarkable talent, not genius" (II, 392). He adds, "extraordinary mental power" in women is "something abnormal" and repels rather than attracts the opposite sex. Therefore, these qualities are diametrically opposed to the will to live (II, 544). In *Essays and Aphorisms,* he notes that appropriate occupations for women are as "nurses and teachers of our earliest childhood precisely because they themselves are childish, silly, and short-sighted, in a word big children, their whole lives long" (81). Woman is a "mental myopic" with "weaker reasoning powers" than men (82). He calls the "veneration of women" in the Christian tradition "ridiculous" (*WWR* II, 431), since women are neither physically nor intellectually appealing in an objective sense; they become *seemingly* attractive only when man is driven by the will to live (i.e., reproduce). Their existence, Schopenhauer states, is for the sole purpose of propagation, and women should "find in this their entire vocation" (*EA* 84). Few writers of the nineteenth century were more blatant in their chauvinism than Schopenhauer.

But before judging him, one must acknowledge that Schopenhauer's views on women differed from many well-respected thinkers of his day only in their unapologetic bluntness. Other less controversial personalities have been pardoned of similar views. More to the point, their entire body of work has not been tainted by the stigma of chauvinism. In other words, Schopenhauer was not out of step with other members of nineteenth century patriarchal "right thinking." Still, Schopenhauer has retained the title of the great misogynist. This reputation, I suggest, stems more from a general rejection of his personality and biography rather than from any unbiased comparison of Schopenhauer's opinions on women with those of his contemporaries.

Schopenhauer felt his view of women justified. Throughout his life women had played only three roles: domineering matriarchs; weak, dependent parasites; or sexual tormentors. The first of these terrified him, the second disgusted and haunted him, and the third enraged him. Womanhood in general had offered nothing positive to Schopenhauer. After his father's death in 1805, his mother Johanna established a successful writing career of her own, entertaining such great minds as Goethe in her home in Weimar. Instead of seeing his mother as an example of female strength, intellect, and independence, the budding philosopher/writer saw her as a threat who possessed the unfair advantage of feminine wiles and manipulative skills to secure the attention and contacts necessary to succeed. Unsure of his own abilities as a scholar and writer, Schopenhauer could not help but view his mother and any woman like her "as an accomplice of the power which threatens self-assertion" (Safranski 138). He also thought his mother's novel writing an embarrassment. For this reason, as well as other personal and financial conflicts, Schopenhauer and his mother ceased to have physical contact with each other in 1814, communicating only through angry letters. In a letter dated 17 May 1814, Johanna cites Arthur's "contempt for [her] sex" as a major reason for her rejection of him (170).

Schopenhauer's "contempt" manifested itself in another, more tragic figure—his sister Adele. If there were ever a concrete example of the hypothetical "Shakespeare's sister" from the literary imagination of Virginia Woolf, Adele Schopenhauer is it. One of Schopenhauer's earliest biographers, W. Wallace, devotes several pages to a discussion of Adele as a writer and thinker potentially equal to her brother. Later biographers discuss her only in relation to her brother, mainly because Adele's literary endeavors, including a collection of short stories based on well-known legends (1844) and a novel, *Anna* (1845), never achieved the recognition of her mother's and brother's work, though they were said "to show taste and grace, rather than power, and to evince considerable skill in narrative" (Wallace 165). More than likely, fiction was not the genre for Adele, though it was a marginally acceptable one for a woman, certainly more appropriate than philosophy. Like her older brother, Adele showed an early sensitivity towards the world, and as she grew she fell victim to the kind of depression Schopenhauer would later call a loss of the will to live.[1] As Wallace comments, "Both brother and sister seem to have had many points in common. Adele, like him, found herself a stranger in life—felt herself cut off from any real intimacy from those around her—and sometimes thought death would not be an unwelcome release from a world that was for her so much an empty show" (166). Unattractive as well as introverted, Adele was often disappointed in love and never married. The only man with whom she attempted to share her innermost thoughts was her brother. Her letters to him reveal a desperate but cautious appeal for help, advice, and consolation. One letter in particular, dated 27 October 1831, reads like an excerpt from one of Schopenhauer's chapters on the process of disillusionment in life:

> Not a single passionate sensation moves me, no hope, no plan—hardly a wish, for my wishes touch on the impossible. Hence I have learned to watch them fly and move away like birds in the blue air. Life displeases me, I have a horror of *old age*, I have a horror of the *lonely life* which is certain my lot. . . . I am strong enough to bear this emptiness, but I should be sincerely grateful to the cholera if it rid me of the whole history without too much violent pain. (Safranski 290)

Cholera did not deliver her from her suffering (she lived to age fifty-two), nor did her brother. Shortly after receiving this letter, Schopenhauer ceased regular communication with her, fearing her financial dependence upon him after their mother experienced a loss a fortune due to poor investments (which Schopenhauer had advised against). Subsequent letters to Schopenhauer from Adele are much more reserved in tone and formal in content. She had been hurt and ignored. Schopenhauer viewed Adele as weak, a potential albatross. Consider the irony of the philosopher who devotes his entire life to freeing people from the burden of feigning bravery in a world which destroys innocence and yet is unable to respond to his own sister's suffering. Even after Adele attempted suicide by jumping from a coach, Schopenhauer took no action to help her. Such insensitivity seems impossible to excuse and difficult to explain, but Safranski suggests that Schopenhauer "resisted being drawn into [Adele's] pitiful life" not out of "hardheartedness but a fear of being drawn into a compassion which, touching as it would on his own depression, would paralyze him." In this sense, Schopenhauer "had a panicky fear of being claimed by Adele" (291). We are left with the image of two individuals struggling to survive desperate depressions, one reaching out for help, the other moving away in order to save himself. [2]

The relationship with his mother and sister formed the basis of Schopenhauer's attitude toward women. He stood little chance as an adult of building strong, healthy attachments to women. Because he viewed them as harpies and parasites, he resented what he believed was their sexual power. He was incapable of seeing lovemaking as anything but a base expression of animal desires over which he had little control. He would later devote much of his philosophy of the will to a discussion of sexual intercourse as the ultimate assertion of the will to live, a hideous act with hideous results. Given this mind set, one would think that Schopenhauer would have been more or less indifferent to the affections of women and even less concerned with their opinion of him. But this is simply not true. In fact, the evidence suggests that although Schopenhauer had many sexual affairs, his inability to find a woman to accept him as a husband was a bitter concern for him and in large part contributed to his misogyny. [3] He once wrote, "I was very fond of [women]—if only they would have had me" (Safranski 67).

One particular woman who ultimately rejected Schopenhauer is responsible for a curious contradiction between his early thoughts on female sexuality and those which appear later in *The World as Will and Representation*. Caroline Richter, a sexually promiscuous actress, so fully captured Schopenhauer's heart in 1822 that despite her infidelities, Schopenhauer remained steadfast in his feelings for her to the end of his life, even remembering her in his will. During his relationship with Richter, Schopenhauer recorded an astounding observation on the absurdity of societal restrictions on female sexuality. His motive was no doubt to justify

Richter's unwillingness to remain faithful to him, but nonetheless a journal entry from 1822 which reveals this opinion is worthy of note: "For a woman, limitation to <u>one</u> during the short time of her flowering and fitness, is an unnatural state. She is expected to save for one what he cannot use and what many others desire from her: and she herself is expected to suffer deprivation at that failure. Think of it!" (Safranski 271).

Schopenhauer apparently did indeed "think of it" further, because in the 1844 edition of *The World as Will and Representation* he went to great lengths to explain the necessity and naturalness of female monogamy and the equally natural tendency in the male towards polygamy (see chapter on Olive Schreiner for a full discussion of this matter). Shortly after his relationship with Richter, Schopenhauer was taken to court and sued for kicking a forty-seven year old seamstress out of his apartment. He paid her damages for the rest of her life. Schopenhauer's opinion of women was not improved by this incident.

Still, towards the end of his life, Schopenhauer experienced another revelation concerning women, though few scholars take note of it. In his later years as his work became recognized and cult followers appeared at his doorstep, Schopenhauer was amazed to find women among his most avid admirers. They wrote him letters, stopped him on the street to ask him questions, and even dedicated poems in his honor. He spent a great deal of time talking to women, discovering in them receptive listeners and well-informed conversationalists:

> At the Englischer Hof he had hour-long conversations with one Gisella Nicoletti from Rome, a Rike von Hasse from Hamburg, and an Ada van Zuylen from Amsterdam. In such company he was able to talk, like a young man in love, about problems of logic such as the identity of A=A. Schopenhauer's image of women began to change. (Safranski 348)

For the first time in Schopenhauer's life, women presented themselves not as adversaries like his mother, or emotional or financial burdens like his sister and the unfortunate seamstress, or as sexual temptations, but rather as intelligent admirers and perceptive thinkers. In short, some of them became his friends.

One of the most satisfying experiences of Schopenhauer's last year came from a friendship with a young sculptress named Elizabeth Ney. She visited him in Frankfurt in the fall of 1959 to sculpt a bust. During the month she worked in his apartment, Schopenhauer was reportedly domestically content, delightfully surprised and sweetened by the young woman's ability to converse intelligently about art and the world in general. According to Safranski, Schopenhauer told a visitor, "She works all day at my place. When I get back from luncheon we have coffee together, we sit on the sofa, and I feel as if we were married" (348). At about the same time, Schopenhauer confessed to yet another female friend, Malwida von Meysenburg, "I have not yet spoken my last word about women. I believe that if a woman succeeds in withdrawing from the mass she grows ceaselessly and more than a man" (348). Schopenhauer died ten months later.

Schopenhauer's misogyny was, like much of his philosophy, a result of his life experiences, a coded way to explain what puzzled him. Most of the women in his life were unsatisfactory by his standards. That his own difficult and eccentric nature should have in any way helped to shape his disasters with women did not—perhaps could not—occur to him. Naturally, when women began to praise his work and treat him with the respect he felt he deserved, his opinion of them changed. Still, no one could have been more astonished than Schopenhauer at women's reaction to his life's work. Because of his ignorance of the female experience and the female soul, Schopenhauer had no way of knowing what sensitive chords were struck in the minds of women by his philosophy of insatiable will, endless longing, and constant struggle. These needs and desires formed the very essence of women's lives, and Schopenhauer's words, more than any others of the time, gave a voice to them, a voice that continued to speak to women throughout the nineteenth and into the twentieth century, as the Schopenhauerian tradition in women's literature proves.

II

The connection between Schopenhauer and women is full of ironies. The first is that a philosophy which categorically excludes women from most of its applications (in education, aesthetics, politics, etc.) should be so appealing to them. A second is that most nineteenth and early twentieth century women writers I have studied in relation to Schopenhauer found their way to Schopenhauer through men and seldom read Schopenhauer before first forming an opinion of him from a decidedly male perspective. In most cases, these men made a great deal of Schopenhauer's views on women, either endorsing or condemning them. But seldom do women writers comment on Schopenhauer's misogyny. Apparently, it simply had to be overlooked by women in order to obtain the gems of knowledge he offered. Perhaps the ultimate irony is that Schopenhauer's fame in England began largely as a result of John Oxenford's article in the *Westminster and Foreign Review* of April 1853, a journal which George Eliot edited. Her excited response to Oxenford's article launched Schopenhauer's long-awaited fame in the country he had always coveted as his home. [4] The review reads, in part:

> Few, indeed, we venture to assert, will be those of our English readers who are familiar with the name of Arthur Schopenhauer. Fewer still will there be who are aware that the mysterious being owning that name has been working for something like forty years to subvert the whole system of German philosophy which has been raised by university professors since the decease of Immanuel Kant, and that, after his long labour, he has just succeeded in making himself heard—wonderfully illustrating how long an interval may elapse between the discharge of the cannon and the hearing of the report. (7)

When Oxenford's "report" was heard in England, the subsequent response established a primary link between Schopenhauer and who was perhaps his first "literary daughter," George Eliot. It also "inaugurated what Schopenhauer caustically dismissed as the 'comedy of fame'" (Safranski 8). Though Schopenhauer considered fame just another "shadow play" of the ego, he anxiously awaited it all of his life. Before the Oxenford article, he decided to leave the future of his work to fate, believing that posterity would see what his contemporaries could not: "Posterity," he wrote, "will raise a monument to me" (242). He pretended to be immune to rejection, having been dismissed by publishers who could not sell his work, embarrassed at universities where his lectures went unattended, and generally ignored by the great thinkers of his day (even Goethe, a close friend of Johanna Schopenhauer, seemed mainly to humor him). Still, Schopenhauer lived long enough to see a group of disciples form around him in the 1840's. He also witnessed with great satisfaction the acceptance of his work by the university system in the late 1850's: the University of Leipzig offered a competition entitled "Exposition and Critique of Schopenhauer's Philosophy" (Safranski 347). After Oxenford's article, Schopenhauer's works were simply easier to find; English translations were more readily available. Readers found his writing style refreshingly clear: Schopenhauer was indeed a good writer, perhaps the best stylist in philosophical writing of his time. Readers with little or no philosophical background could understand him.

Fortuitously, other pioneers were aligning public thought in favor of Schopenhauer's world view. Darwin's *Origin of the Species by Means of Natural Selection*, published in 1859, educated English readers in the doctrines of pessimism and determinism. In fact, Darwin's timing, from Schopenhauer's view, was perfect: Darwin gave scientific credence to the Schopenhauerian call for an acceptance of the world as it is—the new spirit (or anti-spirit, if you will) of realism. As Antonio Aliotta perceptively observed in his 1914 study, *The Idealistic Reaction Against Science*,

> this return to Schopenhauer . . . is closely connected with the spread of the theory of evolution and of energetic conceptions.

> The tendency of every organism to self-preservation—the motive power of the struggle for existence—does, as a matter of fact, approximate closely to Schopenhauer's will to live; hence the derivation of intelligence from instinctive life which Darwinism asserted itself able to prove woke an answering chord in his philosophy. (28)

Darwin's appearance was not the only historical development providing him with his "moment in time." When Schopenhauer completed his *Parerga and Paralipomena* in 1850, "the turning point" had arrived; "Schopenhauer would at last make his breakthrough—but not by himself and not by his own strength: the changed spirit of the age met him half-way" (Safranski 330). Hegel was now passe. The emphasis in philosophy changed from idealism and optimism to an acceptance (i.e. resignation) of the phenomenal world as a final cause. Within the next few decades, Europe—Great Britain in particular—would experience the waning of nineteenth century historicism based on the positivistic hoped-for synthesis of faith, science, and the machine. The age of transition into the twentieth century forced many to embrace a philosophy which more satisfactorily addressed the concerns of modern man as he turned away from the last of the pastoral, unmechanized eras to face the dehumanization of industrialism and world wars. "Thus they were finally united," Safranski observes, "Schopenhauer and his time" (330).

Despite Oxenford's welcome and Darwin's "endorsement," Schopenhauer's reputation woes have never completely vanished. Safranski notes, "Not long before his death Schopenhauer observed: 'Mankind has learned a few things from me which it will never forget.' We have learned from him, but we have also forgotten that we have learned anything from him" (345). He is still regarded by many as a lightweight among philosophers. Over a century after his death, Schopenhauer still does not have a clearly defined niche in the history of ideas in Western civilization. Odd, considering Schopenhauer exerted one of the largest philosophical influences on the literature of England in the latter part of the twentieth century and provided modern writers with a relevant philosophical backdrop for their often dark, pessimistic fictive worlds. A quick glance at a list of major writers in the English literary canon who acknowledged studying Schopenhauer underscores his pervasive presence and undeniable popularity in British intellectual thought. The debt owed by Thomas Hardy and D. H. Lawrence to him, for instance, is well documented. Joseph Conrad's characters are regularly evaluated in terms of Schopenhauerian motivation (Land 70). George Gissing's affinity for Schopenhauer represents in part the philosopher's importance in the development of literary naturalism throughout England and France. George Moore stated in 1889, "I owe much of my mind to Schopenhauer" (Bridgewater 11). Ford Madox Ford's father, Dr. Franz Hueffer, specialized in the study of Schopenhauer and began a magazine, *The New Quarterly*, entirely devoted to him. Leonard Woolf included Schopenhauer's *The World as Will and Representation* in his list of books read in 1903. T. E. Lawrence inherited his extensive knowledge of Schopenhauer from Hardy and Lawrence (O'Donnell 73). T.S. Eliot's interest in concepts of the will led him to a quite natural kinship with Schopenhauer (Kertzer 373).

Of course this list is only a partial one and, noticeably, a male one. This book expands the list to include women writers whose interest in Schopenhauer and whose debt to his world view have been overlooked or simply unknown. George Eliot, Olive Schreiner, Virginia Woolf, and Doris Lessing are among the most powerful, most commanding voices in British literature of the nineteenth and twentieth centuries. Of the many philosophical influences which inform their fiction, the enlightened reader will find vestiges and echoes of Arthur Schopenhauer.

Chapter One, Part One
George Eliot's *Middlemarch*: A Schopenhauerian Shadow Play

Like most English-speaking women who knew of Schopenhauer in the nineteenth century, George Eliot first heard of the German philosopher through men who had read *Die Welt als Wille und Vorstellung*. John Oxenford's 1853 article regarding Schopenhauer's philosophy in the *Westminster Review*, co-edited by Eliot, earned great praise from her. Soon afterwards Eliot's companion for most of the last twenty-five years of her life, George Henry Lewes, read all of Schopenhauer's work between 1867 and 1874, during which time Eliot was writing *Middlemarch*. By 1873, Eliot herself had read Schopenhauer's greatest work (McCobb, "Morality" 321). Surprisingly, the majority of Eliot critics have failed to note Eliot's interest in Schopenhauer. Even the most recent biographical and critical studies by Rosemary Ashton, Rosemarie Bodenheimer, Linda Robertson, Shifra Hochberg, Nancy Cervetti, and Frederick Karl have overlooked Eliot's enthusiasm for Schopenhauer's work. In fact, in his major 1995 study, Karl makes only a passing reference to the Oxenford article, noting that it was "unfortunate" that Oxenford did not read German (131), not adding that Eliot did read German and no doubt read Schopenhauer without the need of translation (Guth 914). Ashton, Hochberg, and Cervetti discuss Eliot's well-known interest in Feuerbach, Comte, Goethe, Heine, and Darwin but never mention Schopenhauer. In the most recent major study of Eliot's life and work, Kathyrn Hughes observes that the Oxenford article was the *Westminster Review*'s "most notable success" but does not venture to suggest that Eliot was in any significant way influenced by her introduction to Schopenhauer.

A rare reference to the link between Eliot and Schopenhauer does appear, however, in a 1980 essay by George Levine. He comments on Eliot's overall mental state during the time she first read Schopenhauer as revealed in her letters and notes that Eliot's *Middlemarch* correspondence is

> marked with a deep new awareness of death. Her experience of the painful dying and death of Lewes's twenty-six year old son, Thornton, haunts almost every letter for a year. Suddenly she is full of consciousness of death's approach and seems almost to welcome it. There is, indeed, a Schopenhauerian quality to these letters. . . ., a recognition that only death of desire can bring peace. (170)

Though Levine is equating two very different Schopenhauerian states—death of desire and death itself—he astutely observes a biographical and philosophical link to the sense of hopelessness and ascetic denial which pervades *Middlemarch* and later even more darkly taints *Daniel Deronda*.

So often seen as a rather cerebral study of middle class England, *Middlemarch* is also a tragic canvas on which is broadly painted the gradual breakdown of the ambition, ideals, and willfulness of nearly every man and woman in the novel. Particularly, it is Eliot's confession of the anguish and futility of the intelligent woman's existence. A letter written during the gestation of *Middlemarch* reveals the weariness of a woman who has struggled into middle age, trying to assert her talents while avoiding the prostitution of her body and intellect, only to find that growing older offers not satisfaction but rather a kind of anesthesia: "My strong egoism has caused me so much melancholy, which is traceable to a fastidious yet hungry ambition, that I am relieved by the comparative quietude of personal cravings which age is bringing" (Levine 170; Eliot, *Letters* 124). Ego, hunger, ambition—these words occur over and over again throughout *Middlemarch*.

Little wonder that Schopenhauer spoke so clearly to Eliot at this time. A glance at the epigraphs which open each chapter, most written by Eliot, reveals Eliot's affinity for Schopenhauerian language and leaves the reader with no doubt of the author's pessimism. In these epigraphs the world "brings the iron" with which man forges his own fetters (58); our "golden hours are turning grey," while they "vainly strive to run" (515); "civil war" divides the soul, "clamorous Needs and Pride" reign, augmented by "hungry rebels" (730); and "wandering woe" eventually pays a visit to everyone (793).

From the first page of the novel, a sense of struggle and disappointment dominates. The parable of St. Theresa sets the stage for Eliot's own "foundress of nothing," Dorothea Brooke, and her tragic journey into the abyss of life. Though some critics such as Robert Liddell suggest that the prelude is "a mistake," emphasizing "too strongly one side of [Dorothea's] nature," (139), two important concepts are introduced in this parable: the intolerance of the world towards gifted women and the option of asceticism. Finding no role for them in an "epic life" which their brilliance and aspirations demand, both St. Theresa and Dorothea attempt to retreat into the private cause of asceticism. Theresa burns with religion, Dorothea with altruism, but to the world "their struggles seemed mere inconsistency and formlessness." Within such an unsympathetic environment, these "ardently willing" souls are often lost:

> Here and there a cygnet is reared uneasily among the ducklings in the brown pond, and never finds the living stream of fellowship with its own oary-footed kind. Here and there is born a St. Theresa, foundress of nothing, whose loving heart-beats and sobs after an unattainable goodness tremble off and are dispersed among hindrances, instead of centering in some long-recognizable deed. (25-26)

Or, as Olive Schreiner would later observe, "a striving and a striving . . . and in the end, nothing," both quite apt paraphrases of Schopenhauer's world view.

In *Religious Humanism and the Victorian Novel* (1965), U. C. Knoepflmacher briefly outlines several Schopenhauerian characteristics in *Middlemarch*. Knoepflmacher focuses on the importance of will and willing throughout the novel, taking the terms out of their connotations associated with Christian theology (i.e., "God's will," "free will") and placing them closer to what he believed was Eliot's intended meaning, given her interest in Darwin and Schopenhauer.[1] He identifies will as "the summation of human actions, the cumulative wills of past and present which make George Eliot's 'irony of events' quite similar to the World-Will of Schopenhauer" (111). Will—its assertion, manifestation, starvation, and resurgences—moves events forward throughout the novel and in many cases takes on coded dimensions in certain signifying characters. As Knoepflmacher illustrates, all of Eliot's characters are at the mercy of their individual wills, "swept along by the inexorable stream of human progress," meaning not Hegelian advancement but simply human continuance:

> Dorothea—the story of whose "errant will" provides the main line of action—and her fellow-seekers for perfection, Lydgate and Ladislaw, are all desirous of higher "effects." Fred and Rosamond Vincy likewise want to make an "impression" on the world. . . . Featherstone and Casaubon hope to affect the lives of their survivors through the provisions made in their last "wills. . . ." And yet, without exception, the wills of all of these characters are blunted. (110)

Middlemarch, then, can be seen as a study of will and its effects on individuals who are quite conscious of its existence (Caleb Garth exclaims at one point in the novel, 'For my part, I wish there was not such thing as a will," voicing, no doubt, the opinion of every individual sentient enough to know when he is trapped [372]).[2] Ultimately Knoepflmacher concludes by suggesting a Schopenhauerian moral in *Middlemarch*, one that women writers influenced by Schopenhauer invariably grasp: an awareness of an obligation to fellow travelers in suffering; "'a consciousness of the not ourselves,' of powers beyond the scope of the individual will, makes for 'righteousness'" (122). This is another way of stating Schopenhauer's belief in sympathy and compassion as the only salvation, the only manner of coping with the will short of asceticism. Critics often note Eliot's emphasis on the theme of sympathy in *Middlemarch* as well as her other novels. As Ellen Argyros observes, "one would be hard-pressed to identify a more important or saturated abstract noun in her lexicon than 'sympathy'" (17). Young Moo-Kim concurs: "'Sympathy' is the most important single word in George Eliot's vocabulary" (42), and she argues that for Eliot, sympathy equals morality (43), seeing as she does society as an "organism," with the individual and society "closely entwined, forming an organic whole" (47). Both critics cite possible sources for Eliot's philosophy: Wordsworth, Comte, Feuerbach, Stowe, Goethe, and German sociologist W. H. Riehl. Only Knoepflmacher heard the echoes of Schopenhauer in Eliot's pleas for a resurrection of human sympathy.

With Knoepflmacher's observation in mind, we find that Eliot's novel lends itself to a new and exciting explication based on the motivating force of the will, the morality of sympathy, and Eliot's certain understanding of Schopenhauer's pessimism. A fictive world based on Schopenhauer's ethics takes shape, with Dorothea assuming the role of the tortured ascetic, and Will signifying the unrestrained, troubling, and seductive *will*. This interpretation offers an explanation for what has traditionally been seen as the greatest flaw in the novel: the dramatic change in Will Ladislaw's character at the end of the novel. The culmination of this narrative pattern is a surprisingly complete representation of Schopenhauer's world of shadows, hopeless struggle, and ultimate defeat, a novel riddled with signs of entrapment (spider webs make frequent appearances) and the struggle of men and women to free themselves of the labyrinth of their existence, only to find themselves further entangled and involved in more desperate struggle.

Though it is tempting to blame Dorothea's marriage to the aging scholar Casaubon for the beginning of her struggle and fall, to do this is to ignore what

Eliot tells us about Dorothea's childhood and upbringing. Dorothea's life of struggle and preordained tragedy was determined at birth by her natural intellect and innate sensitivity, both of which prohibited her from traveling the easier path of subservience and mindless occupation "enjoyed" by her less insightful sisters. "Certainly," Eliot comments, "such elements in the character of a marriageable girl tended to interfere with her lot" (30). The traditional education for homemaking and child-rearing could not satisfy, nor could the half-hearted attempts to feed women bland portions of academics, which Dorothea bitterly refers to as "that toy-box history of the world adapted to young ladies" (112). The longing for knowledge, a hunger as strong as any passion in Dorothea, turned her in directions which seemed logical alternatives to unattainable control over her own happiness: she immersed herself in a religious, altruistic system, entered into an ascetic state of denial of self (an ironic denial, of course, since society had never granted "self" to her in the first place), and embarked on a pilgrimage to find a saint of knowledge and power whom she might worship and martyr herself for:

> The intensity of her religious disposition, the coercion it exercised over her life, was but one aspect of a nature altogether ardent, theoretic, and intellectually consequent: and with such a nature, struggling in the bands of a narrow teaching, hemmed in by a social life which seemed nothing but a labyrinth of petty courses, a walled-in maze of small paths that led no wither, the outcome was sure to strike others as at once exaggeration and inconsistency.
>
> . . . Into this soul-hunger as yet all her youthful passion was poured; the union which attracted her was one that would deliver her from her girlish subjection to her own ignorance, and give her the freedom of voluntary submission to a guide who would take her along the grandest path. . . . "I should learn to see the truth by the same light as great men have seen it by. And then I should know what to do, when I got older." (51)

Her desire for "voluntary submission" is significant. Having realized at a young age that life means submission to a "soul-hunger," Dorothea attempts as she grows older to gain some control over her means of submission. If life means being a victim, then might the individual choose his/her master? After finding the world unwilling to grant her much, Dorothea decides to maintain some kind of control over her own will instead of allowing the world to assert itself upon her. The fact that her submission will be "voluntary," at least in her own mind, is important to her, and it emphasizes for us the pathos of her situation.

As a young girl and adolescent, Dorothea's favorite activity was horseback riding: "she enjoyed it in a pagan sensuous way." She treasured this "indulgence" all the more because she "always looked forward to renouncing it" (32). As she grew into a young lady, her appearance reflected her disdain for worldly adornment, wearing her hair simply, choosing dresses for their practicality, and giving her more elaborate jewelry to her sister. This disregard for the subtleties of fashion, so important to most young women involved in the marriage market of the time, was, Eliot tells us, "a trait of Miss Brooke's asceticism" (49). Even those who admire Dorothea do not understand her habits, which in addition to her stoic appearance include "strange whims of fasting like a Papist" (31) and an intense belief in "that submergence of self in communion with Divine perfection" (47). Sir James Chettam, Dorothea's former beau and constant friend, comments to Dorothea's sister, his future bride, "Your sister is given to self-mortification, is she not?", to which Celia responds with simplicity but no comprehension of the tragedy behind her answer, "She likes giving up" (41). What neither James nor Celia could understand is that Dorothea's asceticism was her only means of escaping her own impossible needs. Her marriage to Casaubon, therefore, shocked both of them tremendously, not seeing that marriage suggested to Dorothea a supreme opportunity for further self-denial while permitting herself, perhaps in the guise of service to another, a glimpse of that bright, forbidden world of knowledge, power, and autonomy inhabited by men.

To satisfy Dorothea's asceticism, marriage must at once involve a sacrifice of self and the betterment of oneself for the good of another. These are not as mutually exclusive as they may first appear. Just as Eliot herself recognized that absorption with self, egoism, can only lead to misery, Dorothea understands that she must discipline her own hungering self, feeding it only with food which will nourish others. What she hopes to gain, then, from her marriage to Casaubon is a submergence of selfish longings and a satisfaction of her altruistic longings for knowledge which might be used to help mankind (starting with her husband). She would remove from her heart the petty whims of youth and immerse herself in the only "cause" available to this new Theresa:

> Something she yearned for by which her life might be filled with action at once rational and ardent; and since the time was gone by for guiding visions and spiritual directors, since prayer heightened yearning but not instruction, what lamp was there but knowledge? Surely learned men kept the only oil; and who more learned than Mr. Casaubon? (112-113)

Serving Casaubon in his "hard struggle," his "lonely labour" (520) as a Miltonic daughter would offer Dorothea the opportunity which her frustrated youth had been seeking, a chance to move "towards the perfect Right, that it might make a throne within her, and *rule the errant will* [italics mine]" (846). For Dorothea, the way to the "perfect Right" is clear: through selflessness, duty to others, productive work, and general sympathy to mankind, one might shed some light on the world's darkness. She explains to Will Ladislaw:

> I have no longings . . . I mean for myself. Except that I should like not to have so much more than my share without doing anything for others. But I have a belief of my own, and it comforts me
> . . . . That by desiring what is perfectly good . . . we are part of the divine power against evil—widening the skirts of light and making the struggle with darkness narrower. (427)

Although the importance of work is a defiant theme in *Middlemarch*, Dorothea's need to be a part of some constructive, intellectually and spiritually satisfying work is not only a feminist or middle-class political statement; it is a theme directly related to her Schopenhauerian desire to escape self, submerging it in activity or objectifying it in work. The tragedy that befalls Dorothea when she fails to find this escape in her marriage to Casaubon must be seen as more than the unfortunate repression of a gifted woman's talents, an all too common story in the nineteenth century. Rather it represents the horrifying entrapment of an individual by her own will and its certain victory over any attempt to thwart it. Its victory over Dorothea's intended cause begins immediately after her marriage to Casaubon. On their honeymoon in Rome, Dorothea realizes that she does not possess the educational tools with which to appreciate the great city's history and art, and her husband has no inclination to give her the keys to his storehouse of knowledge. When they return to Lowick, Dorothea's first great disappointment is that there is not enough for her to do: "She would have preferred, of finding that her home would be in a parish which had a larger share of the world's misery, so that she might have had more active duties in it" (103). Instead of productive work, Dorothea is given only mechanical tasks, such as copying or oral reading, to contribute to her husband's work. The remainder of her time is her own, and she soon begins to feel the torment of her selfhood, her will, growing within her. That "stifling oppression of that gentlewoman's world, where everything was done for her and none asked for her aide" (307) had turned her vision of a marriage based on mutual respect and high ideals into a vacuum:

> "What shall I do?" "Whatever you please, my dear": that had been her brief history since she had left off learning morning lessons and practising silly rhythms on the hated piano. Marriage, which was to bring guidance into worthy and imperative occupation, had not yet freed her from the gentlewoman's oppressive liberty. . . . Her blooming full-pulsed youth stood there in moral imprisonment

> which made itself one with the chilled, colourless, narrowed landscape, with the shrunken furniture, the never-read books, and the ghostly stag in a pale fantastic world that seemed to be vanishing from the daylight. . . .[Dorothea] felt nothing but the dreary oppression. (307-308)

Still, Dorothea could accept this oppression, since after all, such had always been her lot, as long as she could believe in her husband's purpose. She blamed her own "spiritual poverty" for her depression (224), and since "permanent rebellion, the disorder of a life without some loving resolve, was not yet possible to her" (227), she turned her energy towards faith in her husband/father/god for whom she had chosen to sacrifice herself: "in Dorothea's mind there was a current into which all thought and feeling were apt sooner or later to flow—the reaching forward of the whole consciousness towards the fullest truth, the least partial good. There was clearly something better than anger and despondency" (235). This "something better" was not within her female power to create, but perhaps her husband's work would achieve what she could not. Maybe, by being his wife, his pupil, his disciple, she would enjoy vicariously the satisfaction of giving something "good," something true, to the world. Unfortunately, as J. Hillis Miller observes, Dorothea's marriage to Casaubon merely "leads to her discovery that no man can be a god for another in a world without God" (115-116).

Casaubon's role in this shadowy world is unmistakable: he is Schopenhauer's blind ego, the will turned inward, making its fitful way through the task of life only to arrive at the culmination of nothingness. Casaubon's scholastic efforts are essentially meaningless, though the energy expended to create this nothingness is as great as if he were indeed creating a worthwhile piece of criticism. In other words, as Schopenhauer contends, the will is pure motion and being, and the result of its motion and being is irrelevant. Casaubon blindly pursues useless information because he must; this is the manifestation of his diseased will, his "pining hunger" (520). Though Casaubon is seldom considered a sympathetic character, Eliot's authorial voice asserts that he must be seen as a part of the larger picture, not an oddity but rather a certain representation of the potential in all of us for willful egoism. In the end, Casaubon's one sin is not his egoism or his inability to overcome will; it is his refusal to reach outside of his ego to touch his fellow man. Casaubon, "spiritually a-hungered like the rest of us," only deepens his own darkness and the darkness of the world by this refusal to show compassion, according to Schopenhauer's ethics. Eliot's authorial voice shows him the sympathy he denies to others: "For my part," the narrator intrudes, "I am very sorry for him. . . . to be present at this great spectacle of life and never to be liberated from a small hungry shivering self" (314). Egoism only intensifies suffering, according to Schopenhauer; therefore, Casaubon's efforts simply pull him further into the spider web of self. Instead of finding satisfaction and protection in his work, Casaubon's "intellectual ambition which seemed to others to have absorbed and dried him, was really no security against wounds" (455). He dies a bitter, jealous man, leaving his work unfinished—and unnoticed.

Appropriately, Will is the one who reveals to Dorothea the futility of her husband's work, the "fruitless treadmill" of his life (520).[3] For Dorothea, Will ("will") is indeed the force through which she awakens to the truth of her life. When Dorothea discovers the tragic waste not only of Casaubon's energy but her own steadfast faith, she falls into a despondency akin to that which Eliot describes in her letters of the time; a darkness seems to overwhelm Dorothea and lead her willingly towards self-denial or death. "What," Dorothea asks, "could be sadder than so much ardent labour all in vain" (254)? The realization that work could be without purpose paralyzed her: "Like one who has lost her way and is weary, she sat and saw as in one glance all the paths of her young hope which she should never find again" (463). Her will seems broken. Her early ascetic desires to retreat from worldliness reassert themselves; she once again wishes to escape life, but this time in order to heal deep wounds. Her former means of escape fail her: "Books were of no use. Thinking was of no use. . . . There was no refuge now from spiritual emptiness and discontent" (516). Dorothea is caught in the trap Schopenhauer describes as the continual tension between absolute necessity of yearning for survival and the desire to cease yearning, the need to be and the desire to cease to be: "In most cases the Will must be broken by the greatest personal suffering before its self-denial appears. We then see the man suddenly retire into himself, after he is brought to the verge of despair through all the stages of increasing affliction with the most violent resistance" (*WWR* I, 392). When complete self-denial fails, as it usually does, only two options are available: to attempt to objectify the will (usually through some form of aesthetics), thus temporarily quieting its effects on the individual; or to surrender to the continual call of the will and attempt to satisfy, one by one, temporarily, the various needs and hungers life presents. This option, taken by most without realizing a choice has been made, is called living.

Dorothea fails miserably to find any peace in the art which surrounds her, namely painting. In this, Eliot literally echoes Schopenhauer's views on this art form, down to several specific details. For Schopenhauer, painting was a rather unsatisfying medium and seldom offered a means of significantly objectifying the will. Because it is unnecessary for painting to address only the "universal beauty" found in other art forms such as music, it often focuses on the worldliness man wishes to escape. "Painting," Schopenhauer states, "may depict even ugly faces and emaciated figures"; therefore, while we may associate other art forms with an "affirmation of the will-to-live," painting is often associated with "its denial" (*WWR* II, 419). (Readers may recall that Casaubon is chosen to sit for a portrait of Aquinas mainly because the face of the old scholar is so corpse-like.) Denial of the will is not a bad thing in Schopenhauer's view, but it is seldom the objective of the art lover; he usually wants only to be elevated above the misery of the world for awhile until he can regain his strength for battle. A major spokesperson for Schopenhauer's will in *Middlemarch* restates these perceptions. Will Ladislaw tells the German painter Naumann, "Your painting and Plastik are poor stuff.

. . . They perturb and dull conceptions instead of raising them. . . . After all, the true seeing is within; and painting stares at you with an instant imperfection" (222). Dorothea, too, sees the concrete arts as disappointing, observing that "the painting and sculpture may be wonderful, but the feeling is often low and brutal, and sometimes even ridiculous" (252). She also notes, as did Schopenhauer, that the subject matter of painting often emphasizes suffering rather than alleviating it through objectification. Dorothea tries to explain to her uncle why she never appreciated his artwork depicting quaintness and comfort in the lives of poor labourers: "That is one reason why I did not like the pictures here, dear uncle—which you think me stupid about. I used to come from the village with all that dirt and coarse ugliness like a pain within me, and the simpering pictures in the drawing room seemed to me like a wicked attempt to find delight in what is false" (424). Like Schopenhauer, Eliot makes no distinction between art and ethics, and art which fails in its ethical purpose—to ease the burden of life—is offensive.[4] Will accuses Dorothea of a "fanaticism of sympathy" (252) when she expresses the opinion that art should be available, both monetarily and aesthetically, to all people, but sympathy is Dorothea's main concern in all aspects of life, art being no exception. This characteristic saves her from the egoism of other characters in the novel and eventually helps to rescue her from despair.

Part of the process of recovering from a period of depression which, according to Schopenhauer, always precedes the realization that life is endless suffering without possibility for escape, is a moment in which one senses an affinity with all of life, a shared struggle, a unified will. Women writers particularly seem to focus on this part of Schopenhauer's philosophy, perhaps because any group of people which has been kept on the outside will place great value on a sense of community and belonging. An instant of enlightenment through nature is a common technique used by women writers to illustrate a change within a character's internal landscape. Between the period of despair shortly before and after Casaubon's death and the time she discovers her attachment to Will Ladislaw, Dorothea experiences a "spot of time," a "moment" in which she realizes her compassion for mankind is a logical and necessary extension of her undeniable bond to all life and to the life force, the will:

> She opened her curtains, and looked out towards the bit of road that lay in view, with fields beyond, outside the entrance-gates. On the road there was a man with a bundle on his back and a woman carrying her baby; in the field she could see figures moving—perhaps the shepherd with his dog. Far off in the bending sky was the pearly light; and she felt the largeness of the world and the manifold wakings of men to labour and endurance. She was part of that involuntary, palpitating life, and could neither look out on it from her luxurious shelter as a mere spectator, nor hide her eyes in selfish complaining. (846)

This experience shows Dorothea that she will be unable to turn away from the world and her obligations to it. It also sets the stage for the acceptance of the role of Will (will) in her life, helping her to understand her longings:

> It was another or rather a fuller sort of companionship that poor Dorothea was hungering for, and the hunger had grown from the perpetual effort demanded by her married life. . . . she longed for objects who would be dear to her, and to whom she could be dear. She longed for work which would be directly beneficent. . . .today she had stood at the door of the tomb and seen Will Ladislaw receding into the distant world of warm activity and fellowship—turning his face towards her as he went. (516)
>
> Her world was in a state of convulsive change . . . which made her tremulous: it was a sudden yearning of heart towards Will Ladislaw. (532)

> There was always the deep longing which had really determined her to come back to Lowick. The longing was to see Will Ladislaw. She did not know of any good that could come of their meeting: she was helpless; her . . . soul thirsted to see him. (583)

Clearly, Will Ladislaw has the same effect on Dorothea as the individual will itself: he both evokes and represents constant, irrational yearning, and whether the end result of this longing be positive or negative is irrelevant. Dorothea's will both imprisons and emancipates her, strengthens (knowledge of Will's love for her makes her feel "as if she had great deal of superfluous strength" [865]), and stupefies ("She looked [upon seeing Will] as if there were a spell upon her . . . while some intense, grave yearning was imprisoned within her eyes" [865]).

Eliot prepares her readers for Will's allegorical role as the representation of Schopenhauer's will from the point of his introduction. He is immediately associated with the qualities of unrestrained freedom, eccentric genius, hedonistic sexuality, and unpredictability. Mrs. Cadwallader calls Will "a dangerous young sprig . . . a sort of Byronic hero" (415). His physical description emphasizes his unruly hair which, when shaken, makes the young man resemble "an incarnation of the spring whose spirit filled the air–a bright creature, abundant in uncertain promises" (512), and his movements mimic "the manner of a spirited horse" (400). Like a wild horse, Will takes delight in his rebellious nature and flaunts it unapologetically: "I come of rebellious blood on both sides," he explains to his new acquaintances, ". . . I am a rebel: I don't feel bound, as you do, to submit to what I don't like" (415, 427). Will sees himself as set apart from the general throng of mankind, more in tune with the metaphysical:

> Genius, he held, is necessarily intolerant of fetters: on the one hand it must have the utmost play for its spontaneity: on the other, it may confidently await those messages from the universe which summon it to its peculiar work, only placing itself in an attitude of receptivity towards all the sublime. (109)

While awaiting "his call," Will meets Dorothea Brooke, and a strange transformation takes place. The sensuous, hot-blooded, undisciplined Will becomes submissive and docile.

Many critics have pointed to his transformation as a weakness in the novel. In an unsigned 1873 review of *Middlemarch*, Henry James argued that Will's character is "insubstantial" (Edel 261). David Daiches agrees, calling Will "dimly defined," and contends that his marriage to Dorothea "is perhaps the least satisfying thing" in the novel, being simply "a purely symbolic picture of the feminine idealism married to a combination of all the masculine virtues" (1070). Barbara Hardy calls the treatment of Will and Dorothea's love affair "a psychological and structural flaw," observing that Will's masculinity "falters" when confronted with the "Puritan" Dorothea (302, 305). Since these readers have not looked at *Middlemarch* as a manifestation of Schopenhauerian will, they do not see how consistent Will's transformation in the presence of Dorothea is with Schopenhauerian philosophy. The chaotic, irrational will is quieted only by exposure to denial and rejection of its worldly demands. The will is tamed by asceticism; Will is tamed by Dorothea.

Schopenhauer insists that the will must feed off of worldliness, our never ending desires for material, spiritual, and emotional fulfillment. Will Ladislaw similarly functions best in the presence of intense energy: "His nature warmed easily in the presence of subjects which were visibly mixed with life and action, and the easily-stirred rebellion in him helped the glow of public spirit" (501). This accounts as well for the seemingly irrelevant authorial comment on Will's "half artistic, half affectionate" fondness for children (503). Their unrestrained joy and boundless enthusiasm for life is a perfect environment for his own energy. But when Will confronts a denial of all this disorder and random energy, his own power is diminished. When Will first meets Dorothea, "his admiration was accompanied with a chilling sense of remoteness" (424). Here was a force which did not embrace him. Further contact with Dorothea only increased the strangeness Will felt in her presence. Her selflessness, her unworldliness offered him no arena for his own ego. Whenever this ego threatened to assert itself in her presence, Dorothea would extinguish it with a cool blast of saintly dictation. For instance, when Will professes that his love for her is all-encompassing and that his existence would have no meaning without it, Dorothea responds, "That was a wrong thing for you to say, that you would have nothing to try for. If we had lost our own chief good, other people's good would remain, and that is worth trying for" (868). Little wonder the formerly passionate, impulsive Will feels his "paralysis more complete" the closer he moves towards this St. Theresa of Middlemarch (513). Dorothea is the ascetic vehicle for the starvation of this Will, and Eliot draws a clear picture of his gradual emancipation: "Hunger tames us, and Will had been hungry for the vision of a certain form and the sound of a certain voice. Nothing had done instead–not the opera, or the converse of zealous politicians" (860). True to the attributes of Schopenhauer's restless will, Ladislaw's transformation in the presence of Dorothea is far from the flaw so many critics cite: it is a necessary response of a Schopenhauerian will to the force of asceticism.

The union of these two forces results, in the case of Dorothea and Will, not in complete annihilation of Will's strength nor in a failure of Dorothea's ascetic nature. Dorothea experiences a literal renewal of her will to live through her love for Will (the repetition here is intentional), and he is saved from his previously unchanneled wanderings and tendencies towards egoism. Though once again Dorothea attempts to seek satisfaction through the activities of a man, this time she makes certain that these activities are productive and beneficial. Knowing that she will never be allowed into the kingdom of knowledge and power, "feeling that there was always something better which she might have done, if she had only been better and known better" (893), Dorothea directs Will's energies towards the work she envisions but cannot execute:

> Will becomes an ardent public man. . . . Dorothea could have liked nothing better, since wrongs existed, than that her husband should

> be in the thick of a struggle against them, and that she should give him wifely help. Many who knew her, thought it a pity that so substantive and rare a creature should have been absorbed into the life of another, and be only known in a certain cycle as a wife and mother. But no one stated exactly what else that was in her power she ought rather to have done. (894)

Despite the fact that *Middlemarch* ends with the conventional happy ending—a marriage—Dorothea's story remains tragic. As the novel closes, she is still "foundress of nothing," looking back on a life which had given her so little room to grow and so much room in which to do nothing. Though she has entered into a much more satisfying relationship than her marriage to Casaubon, Dorothea as an individual garners very little for her life. Her song remains the same as it was in the epigraph to Chapter One: "Since I can do no good because a woman/Reach constantly at something near it" (*The Maid's Tragedy*, Beaumont and Fletcher). Eliot's last glimpse of Dorothea is a blend of Schopenhauerian pessimism and Darwinian naturalism, summarizing her life as "the mixed result of a young and noble impulse struggling amidst the conditions of an imperfect social state. . . . For there is no creature whose inward being is so strong that it is not greatly determined by what lies outside it" (896).

Many others are caught in the web of this imperfect world, and Eliot's coded narrative on the will can be extended far beyond the Dorothea–Will nexus in almost any direction in the novel. In this Schopenhauerian world where life is gradual process of disillusionment, beginning in hope and ending in defeat, few characters better illustrate this process than Dr. Tertius Lydgate. Lydgate's plotline is most noteworthy because of the Schopenhauerian language Eliot employs to tell his story and is perhaps most representative of what Joseph Wiesenfarth calls Eliot's amplification of "the dark side of respectability" in *Middlemarch* (78). From his first appearance, Lydgate is associated with the human struggle; he plans to dedicate his life to the investigation of the physical and emotional impulses which make man what he is. Lydgate is, in essence, a student of the will:

> He wanted to pierce the obscurity of those minute processes which prepare human misery and joy, those invisible thoroughfares which are the first lurking-places of anguish, mania, and crime, that delicate poise and transition which determine the growth of happy or unhappy consciousness. (194)

But while attempting to remain an impartial observer of the chaos of living, Lydgate finds himself in the middle of tension on almost every level. He "felt himself struggling for Medical Reform" while "becoming more and more conscious of the national struggle" for political reform (499).

And there is tension closer to home as well. The central struggle in Lydgate's life is his marriage, though as with Dorothea's tragic marriage to Casaubon, it is too easy to blame the spouse for all the misery. True, Rosamond is a superficial parasite, but Lydgate himself is guilty from the outset of the novel of a general lack of sympathy for anything outside of his specific interests. He chooses Rosamond for his bride—or, rather, is drawn to her—expressly because of her inability to interfere with the closed world he had built for himself. When he later accuses her of being like a basil plant which "flourishes wonderfully on a murdered man's brains" (893), one might rightly ask, "What other food was she given on which to feed?" Not unlike Casaubon, Lydgate had no intention of engaging in a marriage of equals. [5] His requirements for a wife seem to have more to do with her woman-child sexuality and role as a vulnerable creature in an evil world (Lydgate's earlier liaison with an actress who murders her husband attests to his attraction to the romantic and his desire to serve as protector of the weak and injured) than with any sense of equality. He decidedly does not want a woman like Dorothea who "did not look at things from the proper feminine angle." He would find a marriage with such a woman to be a constant challenge as opposed to a "paradise with sweet laughs for bird-notes, and blue eyes for a heaven" (122). Much later

Lydgate would realize what a comfort a woman might be who could act as "a fountain of friendship towards men," a woman of substance who could be a confidant in times of trouble (826). But while still caught up in his egoism, Lydgate sees no need for a woman to act in any other capacity than as a complement to his existence. Rosamond is a perfect complement, being quite incomplete on her own: "she appeared to be that perfect piece of womanhood who would reverence her husband's mind after the fashion of an accomplished mermaid" (628). Unfortunately, mermaids have little understanding of money and even less patience with poverty. When Lydgate finds himself beneath the "vile yoke" of debt, seeking an escape through gambling and opium, he is completely alone (698). He begins his Schopenhauerian descent—his process of disillusionment—with the knowledge that he must walk his path without a companion, partly because Rosamond had never been included in his professional journeys before, and partly because she too lacks the sympathy and selflessness to be of any comfort on such a journey: "The first great disappointment had been borne: the tender devotedness and docile admiration of the ideal wife must be renounced, and life must be taken up on a lower stage of expectation, as it is by men who have lost their limbs" (702). The spiritually maimed Lydgate is drawn more deeply into the web of his own making as the novel progresses, and Eliot's entrapment imagery is never more obvious: Lydgate's marriage "held him as with pincers" (718); his "self was being narrowed into the miserable isolation of egoistic fears and vulgar anxieties" (698); his debt to Bulstrode is likened to a "torture screw" (767); and his final resolve to surrender his idealism and do the world's bidding is "the sort of shell I must creep into and try to keep my soul alive in" (825). Ultimately, Lydgate, having "set out, like Crusaders of old, with a glorious equipment of hope and enthusiasm," is reduced to a broken pawn of the world who views himself as a failure and "all life as one who is dragged and struggling amid the throng" (890, 819). Eliot's Schopenhauerian pessimism is never heard more clearly.

Eliot's suspicion of egoism as the cause of so much of the world's woe is further reinforced by her treatment of various minor characters in *Middlemarch* who manage to escape the trap of selfish individualism and are rewarded with satisfactory, though by no means painless, lives. The Garths are an example. Caleb Garth, we remember, devoutly wishes (in his double entendre) that there were no such thing as a will. Indeed, he lives his life as if his wish had been granted, accepting his poverty and life of labor as his fate and finding beauty in the world nonetheless: "There was no spirit of denial in Caleb, and the world seemed so wondrous to him" (284). Mrs. Garth, too, "had that rare sense which discerns what is unalterable, and submits to it without murmuring" (274), thereby escaping pointless struggle. Neither Caleb's nor his wife's submission appears tragic, however; their lives are filled with an awareness of each other's needs, much human warmth and companionship, and most important, work which satisfies them and benefits others. Their daughter, Mary, inherits her parents' ability to accept that which cannot be changed, as well as their intense work ethic. Out of both she emerges as Eliot's signifying example of sympathy and Schopenhauer's concept of correct submission: the world cannot blackmail her because it has nothing she cannot refuse. [6]

> Having early had strong reason to believe that things were not likely to be arranged for her peculiar satisfaction, she wasted no time in astonishment and annoyance at that fact. And she had already come to take life very much as a comedy in which she had a proud, nay, a generous resolution not to act the mean or treacherous part. (349)

Because of this resolution, Mary is able to love the flighty, irresponsible Fred Vincy while resisting his marriage proposals until he understands his obligation, as she does, to surrender self and ego for the betterment of others. She chastises him: "How can you bear to be so contemptible, when others are working and striving, and there are so many things to be done—how can you bear to be fit for nothing in the world that is useful?. . . You must love your work. . . . You must be proud of your work" (288, 606). Like her father who avoids entangling himself in corruption simply by walking away from a job financed by Bulstrode, Mary has the ability to smell life's traps and thereby avoid them. Marriage to irresponsible Fred would lead to poverty, suffering, and resentment, so she waits until he proves himself before agreeing to share his life. She refuses to destroy Featherstone's will, "against her will," regardless of the outcome, because she innately senses the potential for moral entrapment (442). Eliot's message is clear: if an individual remains indifferent to much of the world's temptations, if he focuses his energy (will) on beneficent work and the welfare of others, his path in life, though not without hardship, will be smoother than if he were immersed in ego and ambition.

Chapter One, Part Two
George Eliot's *Daniel Deronda*: A Study in Schopenhauerian Morality

By the time George Eliot wrote her last novel, *Daniel Deronda*, she had read most if not all of Schopenhauer's major work, *The World as Will and Representation*. Two entries in her manuscript notebooks specifically mention reading Schopenhauer in September of 1872 (McCobb, "*Daniel Deronda*" 535). G. H. Lewes had also continued to expand his knowledge of the German philosopher, ultimately including Schopenhauer in his philosophical publications throughout the late 1860's and early 1870's (McCobb, "Knowledge" 125). G. E. McCobb is the only Eliot scholar who has attempted to illustrate the effect of this considerable exposure to Schopenhauer's philosophy on Eliot's last work. In two articles published during the past decade, McCobb has explored the Schopenhauerian treatment of music and will in *Daniel Deronda*. In the first article, "The Morality of Musical Genius: Schopenhauerian Views in *Daniel Deronda*," McCobb notes the repeated connection in the novel between music and the moral fiber of Eliot's characters, a connection which argues for the superiority of individuals who create great music and those who appreciate its beauty. Those who cannot do either are, in Schopenhauer's view, morally suspect. In his second, more inclusive article, "*Daniel Deronda* as Will and Representation: George Eliot and Schopenhauer," McCobb attempts to isolate some of the major Schopenhauerian themes at work throughout *Daniel Deronda*, including the tension between ego and sympathy, the entrapment of the will, and the potential escape through asceticism. As significant as McCobb's work is, he does not move beyond a recognition of the similarity between these themes and Schopenhauer's views to an overall assessment of Schopenhauerian morality in *Daniel Deronda*.

Though all of Eliot's fictional works are set in worlds partly inhabited by the petty, evil, and lost, *Daniel Deronda* is exceptional in its intense darkness. Unlike previous novels, it plays itself out in internal shadow, that is, in an environment shaped largely by the psychological motivations of its characters. The desperate pessimism which pervades the novel stems not from peripheral circumstances, such as a devastating codicil to a hidden will or a corrupt social system. Rather, it comes from the individual's own worst nature, his inability to overcome the negative influences of the will. Lest there should be any doubt of the source of this evil, lest the reader should entertain the idea that the blame for the maladies about to unfold rests anywhere but with individual impotence in the face of self, Eliot provides the following as her opening epigraph:

> Let thy chief terror be of thine own soul;
> There, 'mid the throng of hurrying desires
> That trample o'er the dead to seize their spoil,
> Lurks vengeance, footless, irresistible
> As exhalations laden with slow death,
> And o'er the fairest troop of captured joys
> Breathes pallid pestilence. (32)

Daniel Deronda concerns itself, then, with the struggle between the various torments associated with egoism and the difficulty of the denial of self. This is the Schopenhauerian condition of life. Schopenhauer's will is present in both states, forcing the individual always into a trap of his own making. The condemnation of ego as the source of human unhappiness is, as seen in *Middlemarch*, a common theme in Eliot's work, as is her endorsement of a life of generosity as a remedy for egoism. In *Daniel Deronda*, however, Eliot sets into motion "this devil's game" which pits individuals against themselves in a desperate battle with their own desires, and the possibility of gaining a winning hand through compassion and sympathy seems left to wistful chance (455). The repeated images of hell and damnation throughout the novel create a fallen world of deepest pessimism and hopelessness, a gambling den of vice and misery, a Schopenhauerian reality.

Within this darkness walks Daniel Deronda, the character Eliot created in an attempt to breathe life into what she saw as the dying embers of human compassion. Deronda is arguably Eliot's most complex character: he is at once self-aware and selfless, searching for identity while trying to deny the self. Unlike Dorothea of *Middlemarch*, Deronda is perfectly cognizant of the Schopenhauerian choice before him: he may strive to satisfy the needs of self or sublimate the self to the welfare of others. He is also fully aware that either choice will result in suffering. His capacity for self-doubt makes him a fuller, less codified character than Dorothea, and he is also a more accurate representation of the Schopenhauerian dilemma. Unlike Dorothea's certain though ultimately tragic understanding of her role as a sympathetic victim, Deronda's sensitivity to others' needs is born of a sympathy for self: he is not at all comfortable with the demands of martyrdom. Though Eliot states that Deronda's "fervour of sympathy" is innate, a product of an "early-wakened sensibility," the adult Deronda struggles with the implications of a life spent in conflict with self (218, 215). He often contemplates "whether it were worth while to take part in the battle of the world" (225). Even after he decides to enter this battle—for the sake of the Mirahs and Gwendolyns of the world—he knows that by aligning himself with the not-self against the willful ego he has placed himself in the role of "the calf" at the mercy of "the butcher" (428, 218).

> A too reflective and diffusive sympathy was in danger of paralysing in him that indignation against wrong and that selectness of fellowship which are the conditions of moral force. . . . He had become so keenly aware of this that what he most longed for was either some external event or some inward light, that would urge

> him into a definite line of action, and compress his wandering energy. (413)

Like the Christ of Gesthemane who asks for the cup of poison to be passed from his lips, Deronda is uncertain in his mission and fearful of the price it must exact from him. Eliot's ambivalence about the price of selflessness is heard throughout the novel. Sir Hugo warns Deronda, "My dear boy, it is good to be unselfish and generous; but don't carry that too far . . . you must know where to find yourself" (224). Mirah likens Deronda's self-sacrifice to "Bouddha giving himself to the famished tigress to save her and her little ones from starvation." Mirah adds, "That is what we all think of you" (522). Since the self is the means of propagating all worldly evil, the annihilation of self for others is an admirable accomplishment in Schopenhauer's moral sense, but Eliot clearly fears loss of individuality. More than in any other novel, Eliot seems concerned with the individual in *Daniel Deronda* and sees the choice of morality over the needs of self as a choice for one type of suffering over another. The Schopenhauerian choice, Eliot realizes, is no choice at all: life is indeed suffering and there is no end to it.

In her world of lost souls, Eliot's reluctant, introspective messiah acts as a magnet for all suffering, "loving too well the losing causes of the world":

> Persons attracted him. . .in proportion to the possibility of his defending them, rescuing them, telling upon their lives with some sort of redeeming influence; and he had to resist an inclination
> . . .to withdraw coldly from the fortunate. (413, 369)

The fire of all compassion feeds off of need, and various victims of the insatiable will seek purification and peace through Deronda's benevolent flame. Gwendolyn and Mirah both become disciples of Deronda, and they find in him what Schopenhauer asserts will be found in a life of selflessness: an escape from the trap of life's misery.

Gwendolyn eventually turns Deronda "into a priest" (485) after she loses herself in the games of her life. From her first appearance Gwendolyn is portrayed as a willful egoist, determined to win in her gamble to control her own destiny. As a disenfranchised woman, the odds are greatly against her spiritual survival, but Gwendolyn is so immersed in self, in her own blind willfulness, that the possibility of a larger force beyond her dominance is unfathomable to her. From marriage to wealth to happiness in general, she believed "her will was peremptory" (46), and "felt well-equipped for the mastery of life" (69). Early in the novel she asks rhetorically, "What is the use of my being charming if it is to end in my being dull and not minding anything? . . . I will not put up with [marriage] if it is not a happy state. I am determined to be happy—at least not to go on muddling away my life as other people do, being and doing nothing remarkable" (58). Determined to escape the fate of her life-worn mother, she sees the need for power and control over her own actions: "other people allowed themselves to be made slaves of, and to have their lives blown hither and thither like empty ships in which no will was present: it was not to be so with her" (69). Her mother attempts several times to illustrate through words and example the futility of fighting life's random blows. Once when Gwendolyn considers a part in a play as Saint Cecilia, she complains, "Mine is only a happy nose; it would not do so well for tragedy," to which her mother replies, "Oh, my dear, any nose will do to be miserable in this world" (57). Still, Mrs. Davilow finds her daughter's "will . . .always too strong," calling Gwendolyn "sensitive because she did not like to say wilful" (129, 176). Despite her mastery and willfulness, Gwendolyn is not blind to her mother's living example of the fate of most women. Because of this, Gwendolyn fears more than anything else subjugation and restraint:

> We women can't go in search of adventures. . . . We must stay where we grow, or where the gardeners like to transplant us. We are brought up like the flowers, to look as pretty as we can, and be dull without complaining. That is my notion about the plants: they are often bored, and that is the reason why some of them have got poisonous. (171)

Gwendolyn herself is already infected with the poison of egoism which will eventually destroy her. Her "inborn energy of egoistic desire" leads her to repeated gambling, both literal and metaphorical (71). She is wagering her money and jewels at the gambling table when Deronda first meets her, and soon after she wagers her autonomy in a tragic marriage designed for profit. Still unable to relinquish the illusion of control over her own will, she announces to her mother, "If I am to be miserable, let it be my own choice" (192). After Gwendolyn's rude awakening to the world's cruelty, that is, after her family's financial misfortune, she immediately perceives her impotence, and naturally gravitates towards a source of power. Her marriage to Grandcourt is more a result of this realization than of poverty. Though she feared Grandcourt's "subjugation of her will" (168), and though the opportunities of marriage to him "had come to her hunger like food with the taint of sacrilege upon it" (356), she found in Grandcourt someone whose will indeed seemed indestructible. Under the protection of this will and, admittedly, domination, she could regain some of her shaken control over the malevolent whims of the world:

> Gwendolyn's will had seemed impervious . . . but it was the will of a creature with a large discourse of imaginative fears: a shadow would have been enough to relax its hold. And she found [in Grandcourt] a will like that of a crab or a boa-constrictor which goes on pinching or crushing without alarm at thunder. (477)

Of course, instead of being protected or emancipated by this will, Gwendolyn becomes its victim: "she had neither devices at her command to determine his will, nor any rational means of escaping it" (480). Her marriage is her "last great gambling loss" (496) and serves as verification of what Gwendolyn's mother had warned: life in its procession crushes all, most ruthlessly those who will not submit easily to its power.

If Gwendolyn was in need of being taught a lesson by the world, Grandcourt was to be her teacher. He would show her how to desire and fail, bend and break.

Grandcourt's main function in the novel is to tame Gwendolyn's egoism at the cost of her spirit and pride, much in the manner of his beloved hunting practices. Gwendolyn makes the observation: "He delights in making the dogs and horses quail: that is half his pleasure in calling them his. . . . It will come to be so with me; and I shall quail" (482). Conquest being the main motivation behind his marriage to Gwendolyn, Grandcourt's interest in his wife soon becomes one of possession and dominance, as his wife prophesied. Having lived all of his life "without the luxury of sympathetic feeling" (479), Grandcourt has no sense of Gwendolyn's needs. He sees her exclusively as an acquisition to be controlled and his marriage as the means through which "new objects to exert his will upon" had been brought into his life (645). Gwendolyn awakens from her dream of a protected, safe life to find that the man she had once half-seriously likened to a "handsome lizard" has become "a dangerous serpent ornamentally coiled in her cabin without invitation" (174, 735).

What happens to Gwendolyn after she realizes her complete defeat in marriage is similar to the kind of depression and despair Schopenhauer describes as part of the process of self-annihilation: once man accepts his own impotence in the face of will, he must know that he is nothing as an individual and that his ego is a sham. What ensues then is a world-weariness, a turning away from all that once defined life: food, ambition, work, comradeship. Suicide enters the mind as a welcome form of escape. As Schopenhauer points out, however, the act of suicide requires a great deal of ego and will which the truly defeated individual no longer possesses. Gwendolyn for the first time finds herself living in limbo: "It was not in her nature to busy herself with the fancies of suicide . . . . What occupied and exasperated her was the sense that there was nothing for her but to live in a way she hated" (318). Her "appetite had sickened" (484); she "felt a sort of numbness and could set about nothing" (317-318). Her overall state is described as "a world-nausea," and a "sick motivelessness," a result of her observation that "there was really nothing pleasant to be counted on in the world"

(317-318).

As McCobb notes, Deronda "is a logical counterpart to Gwendolyn" and the dangers of egoism which she represents ("*Daniel Deronda*" 513). Whereas Gwendolyn's life of selfishness and materialism leads her to the brink of destruction, Deronda's selflessness buoys him throughout his own trials as well as enables him to save others. What he prescribes for the lost Gwendolyn is not a rediscovery of self but rather a Schopenhauerian commitment to the not-self, and immersion not in the world but in the concerns of the other. By denying one's own desires and needs in favor of the betterment of others, one might find, according to Schopenhauer and Eliot, some relief from the inferno of willfulness. "Look on other lives beside your own," Deronda advises Gwendolyn, "See what their troubles are, and how they are borne. Try to care about something in this vast world besides the gratification of small selfish desires . . . something that is good apart from the accidents of your own lot" (501-502). In order to enter into this state of sympathy, Gwendolyn must first initiate a change in her defensive character and learn submission, something she has always feared. But as Schopenhauer states, submission to the yoke of the world is the fate of all mankind, and turning this submission into service to others is the only good. To make one's own "unalterable wrong a reason for more effort towards a good that may do something to counterbalance the evil" is the only morality in a fallen world (*Daniel Deronda* 506). Ultimately Deronda suggests to Gwendolyn a most drastic step in her personal evolution, a Schopenhauerian choice suggested earlier in *Middlemarch*: religious asceticism. Deronda explains to Gwendolyn, "The refuge you are needing from personal trouble is the higher, the religious life, which holds an enthusiasm for something more than our own appetites and vanities" (507-508). Note that Deronda does not suggest religion as a means of achieving heavenly reward or immortality. Like Schopenhauer, Deronda sees the primary virtue of religion as the escape it affords one from the demands of the world, an ascetic alternative. Deronda himself is on a pilgrimage towards spiritualism, not, as some critics suggest, to establish some kind of haven of Judaism but rather to arrive at a place free of the constant searching which has made up his life thus far.

At the end of the novel it is uncertain as to whether Gwendolyn will be successful in her own pilgrimage and her efforts to subjugate ego to the not-self. True asceticism seems unlikely for Gwendolyn. Perhaps this ambiguity is due in part to Eliot's own rejection of the "ascetic dissolution of self which [Schopenhauer] considers the logical outcome of sympathy," as McCobb suggests ("*Daniel Deronda*" 543). Certainly the possibility of losing one's self is frightening to Eliot, as seen her ambivalent treatment of Dorothea's character. But Gwendolyn does make definite moves away from an all-encompassing will, entering into "the struggling regenerative process" to which Deronda had introduced her (841). Instead of the dreadful death of her soul which she experienced after her marriage, this last surrender of will brings to Gwendolyn "that peaceful melancholy which comes from the renunciation of demands for self" promised by Schopenhauer (866). Her final commitment to Deronda "to be one of the best women, who make others glad they were born" (882) places Gwendolyn firmly in the company of Eliot's other selfless Saint Theresa, Dorothea Brooke, though the means of Gwendolyn's salvation remain uncertain as the novel closes.

As many critics have pointed out, Gwendolyn also shares several characteristics with Rosamond Vincy of *Middlemarch*. Aside from the obvious similarities of egoism and coquetry, both women are indeed "poisonous plants" to the idealistic men who enter their realms. Lydgate offers himself up in sacrifice to Rosamond's needs and receives only a cold, forfeited marriage in return. Eliot realizes that Gwendolyn, though redeemed at the end of the novel, would also suffocate the saintly Deronda with her bottomless desires. Had Deronda taken on the role of husband to Gwendolyn, he would surely have fallen victim to the loss of individualism which Eliot saw as the price of total selflessness. Gwendolyn needed all that Deronda could give for her salvation, and then some.

Mirah, however, is Deronda's salvation. As selfless, as removed from worldly expectations as Deronda, she is, literally, his soulmate. Therefore, she takes nothing from him, and she is able to contribute to his quest for wholeness and identity. Like Gwendolyn, Mirah represents Schopenhauerian suffering saved by compassion. But unlike Gwendolyn, and more akin to *Middlemarch*'s Mary Garth, Mirah has already learned submission to the will and the benefits of denying self. Eliot informs her readers shortly after introducing Mirah that "it is not in her nature to run into planning and devising: only to submit" (265). Suffering was no stranger to Mirah, and therefore she never felt outrage or astonishment when it visited her:

> Those who have been indulged by fortune and have always thought of calamity as what happens to others, feel a blind incredulous rage at the reversal of their lot, and half believe that their wild cries will alter the course of the storm. Mirah felt no such surprise when familiar Sorrow came back. (800)

When Deronda first encountered Mirah, she had resigned herself to hopelessness and suicide. Though Schopenhauer recognizes suicide as a seemingly logical solution to an individual's irrational, senseless suffering, he explicitly points out the uselessness of this act in destroying the will, the source of all suffering. Thoughts of suicide are simply part of the process of disillusionment. But those who, like Mirah, actually attempt suicide have been deceived by the will itself, Schopenhauer explains: the taking of one's own life requires a tremendous assertion of the will rather than its denial. The will is never stronger than in the act of suicide: instead of denying one's inextricable bond to the world and all of its pain, suicide demonstrates the strength of the inescapable chains of life. The will itself is not destroyed through suicide but instead continues on in a more powerful, virulent form.

Though Schopenhauer's views on suicide are among his most complex and controversial, Eliot reveals a fine understanding of them in her description of

Mirah's attempted suicide. Early in the novel, Eliot prepares her reader for Mirah's act by linking desperation and will: "Moments of suffering . . take the quality of action, like the cry of Prometheus, whose chained anguish seems a greater energy than the sea and the sky he invokes and the deity he defies" (202). Eliot clearly sees Mirah's action as a similar cry of desperation in the face of life's misery, "the 'maggior dolere' and the 'miseria'" having overtaken "the 'tempio felice'," as Mirah explained (233). Eliot also sees the suicide as part of the process of subjugation to the world's power. She explicitly demonstrates her understanding of Schopenhauer's perception of the role of the will in suicide through Mirah's motivation:

> [Life] seemed all a weary wandering, and heart-loneliness. . . . I had a terror of the world. . . . always before I had some hope; now it was gone. . . . I could only feel what was present in me—it was all one longing to cease from my weary life . . . *And a new strength came into me to will what I should do. . . . I was going to die* [italics mine]. (263-64)

Schopenhauer would observe here that Mirah is well on her way to denial of the will in her lost, hungry, cold state of hopelessness, but the will reasserts itself in her thoughts of suicide: the weak, broken woman disappears and a "new strength" enabling her "to will what [she] would do" takes over. Far from seeing suicide as a passive surrender to death by a world-beaten individual, Eliot paints a Schopenhauerian portrayal of suicide as the defiant cry of the will through an individual who is striving one more time to "battle the world."

What saves Mirah from this misguided attempt to escape the will is the same power which might give comfort to us all, according to Schopenhauer: human compassion. For Mirah, this comes in the personage of Deronda: "Some ray or other came—which made her feel that she ought to live. . . . She is full of piety and seems capable of submitting to anything when it takes the form of duty" (494). Compassion, submission, duty to others, these form the essence of

Schopenhauerian morality. Mirah and Deronda embrace these characteristics in order to channel the ambition of the individual will in charitable directions. And they clearly speak Eliot's message to the world. In her 1999 study of Eliot, Kathryn Hughes paraphrases the author's response to those who sought her advice on how to survive unhappiness: "Always she told them the same thing—resign yourself to suffering, wean yourself off the hope of a future life, and nourish your fellow feeling towards the men and women you encounter every day" (280). This, Schopenhauer would respond, is the best we can do.

Central to Schopenhauerian morality is the understanding of man's link to all things by and through the will. Our being, our worldly state, our means of existence stem from the same source—the will. Knowing this not only increases our capacity for sympathy and compassion for other human beings but also provides a sense of belonging, of wholeness, with the universe, the past and future, and all internal and external landscapes. Even suffering is diminished by an awareness of its being shared. Mirah, for example, finds strength in the realization that her pain links her to the past and the future: "It comforts me to believe that my suffering was part of the affliction of my people, my part in the long song of mourning that has been going on through ages and ages" (256). Deronda, too, is quite aware of his oneness with all people and all things. He is, Eliot tells us, one of "the rarer sort, who presently see their own frustrated claim as one among a myriad" (215). He had "the habit of seeing things as they probably appeared to others" (412). This echoes Schopenhauer on the subject of virtue: "Virtue must spring from the intuitive knowledge that recognizes in another's individuality the same inner nature as one's own" (*WWR* I, 367-68). Nature, too, mirrored Deronda's self, providing him an opportunity to enter into a state where inner and outer will seem identical: he could forget everything "in a half-speculative, half-involuntary identification of himself with the objects he was looking at, thinking how far it might be possible habitually to shift his center till his own personality would be no less outside him than the landscape" (229). Like the music Deronda loves, nature not only offers an escape from the will but also acts as a Schopenhauerian representation of it. [1] A beautiful evening to Deronda is "an unfinished strain of music," somber dusk a time "when thinking and desiring melt together imperceptibly" (220). [2] A supreme example of Schopenhauerian compassion and morality, Deronda perceives the will, both his own and the world's, as "a sublimely penetrating life, as in the twin green leaves that will become the sheltering tree" (414-15). He is perfectly aware of the Schopenhauerian distinction between the idea or representation of a thing and the thing-in-itself, the life force within or behind the false representation. This awareness saves him much suffering in the cruel "shadow play" of life. This is the comfort Schopenhauer hoped to give the world, the knowledge that all aspects of life, including its moments of deepest suffering, are temporary, fleeting shadows of the eternal. These representations are not to be grieved over. All things pass, all things fade away, except the will, which is indestructible. Though neither Deronda nor Mirah enters into the fatalism which must follow a complete acceptance of Schopenhauer's world view, they do embark on a journey of the spirit at the end of the novel, seeking the peace found in the renunciation of worldliness.

Chapter Two

"A Striving and a Striving": Schopenhauerian Pessimism in Olive Schreiner's *The Story of an African Farm* and *From Man to Man**

In a letter dated 2nd March 1885, Olive Schreiner wrote the following to her friend Havelock Ellis:

> I have been looking at that life of Schopenhauer today. If I had ever read him, or even knew before I came to England that such a man existed, one would say I had copied whole ideas in the *African Farm* and *From Man to Man* from him. There is one passage of his on the search for philosophic truth that reads like a paraphrase of my allegory in the *African Farm*. There's something so beautiful in coming on one's very most inmost thoughts in another. In one way it's one of the greatest pleasures one has. That Life by Miss Zimmern is very well written. (*Letters* 61).

---

*Sections of this chapter were previously published in *English Literature in Transition* 37:3 (Sept. 1994): 303-16.

Schreiner mentions Schopenhauer two more times in extant letters, both again addressed to Ellis. In one she expresses a desire to read some Schopenhauer while she recovers from a recurring illness: "I wish so much I could have Schopenhauer. I begin to feel I want to read, not much, only now and then a few words. All relating to Socialism interests me" (6 April 1887, *Letters* 113). The other simply alludes to Schopenhauer in passing, a reference to Schopenhauer's sexual nature hinted at in Zimmern's biography: "this celibacy has not been good for me. . . . I mean that I am sure celibacy is not good for the brain of a continual [brain-worker]. Schopenhauer, Goethe, Shakespeare, no really great, steady thinker has ever been celibate" (27 Jan 1888, *Letters* 130). Despite these references, the most recent biography of Schreiner by Cherry Clayton (1997) makes no reference to her interest in Schopenhauer. Ruth First and Ann Scott in their 1980 biography do address Schreiner's identification with Schopenhauer and claim that Schreiner actually "read Schopenhauer's work and a *Life* during the eighteen-eighties" (61). More likely, Schreiner's basic knowledge of Schopenhauer came from two secondary sources: Zimmern's greatly simplified, incomplete study of Schopenhauer's life and philosophy,[1] and the observations of Schreiner's husband and literary tutor, S. C. Cronwright, who specifically mentions in his biography of Schreiner discussions with his wife about various philosophers, including Schopenhauer.

Despite a lack of access to primary material, Schreiner was indeed correct in her awareness of a kinship with Schopenhauer. *The Story of an African Farm* reads like a narrative offspring of *The World as Will and Representation*. True, *African Farm* predates Schreiner's reading of Zimmern's study as well as her discussions with Cronwright, but apparently she intuitively "knew" Schopenhauer's will, his pessimism, and his world view long before *African Farm* was conceived. Despite the fact that Schopenhauer's philosophy excludes any possibility of female greatness and artistry (something Zimmern downplays in her work), Schreiner's joy in discovering that one of the great minds of the nineteenth century verified her own experiences and insights is understandable. *African Farm* had met its share of harsh criticism, based mostly on its darkness and its lack of sensational action (action, expected, perhaps, because of Schreiner's use of the male pseudonym, Ralph Iron, under which the novel first appeared): one critic suggested "he would better have liked the little book if it had been a history of wild adventure . . . 'of encounters with ravening lions, and hair-breadth escapes'" (Schreiner, Preface to Second Edition, 1883, *African Farm* viii). But Schreiner had another story to tell, as she tried to explain:

> This could not be. Such works are best written in Piccadilly or in the Strand; there the gifts of the creative imagination, untrammeled by contact with any fact, may spread their wings. But, should one sit down to paint the scenes among which he has grown, he will find that the facts creep in upon him. . . . Sadly he must squeeze the color from his brush, and dip it into the gray pigments around him. He must paint what lies before him. ("Preface" viii, ix)

Schreiner might have added "and within him," for "within" is where the darkness exists in her novel, and it emanates from her characters, tainting the outside world. Discovering Schopenhauer enabled Schreiner to dismiss the critics who requested more color, knowing now that she had used the only color appropriate for the world both she and Schopenhauer envisioned.

African Farm is the story of Waldo (in part representing Schreiner herself remembering her childhood on the South African Plains) and his education into the African world. This education takes the form of a process of disillusionment, as all of our experiences must, according to Schopenhauer: "We shall do best to think of life as a desengano, as a process of disillusionment; since this is, clearly enough, what everything that happens to us is calculated to produce" (*Essays* 54). *African Farm* is as detailed in the treatment of this process as Schreiner is in the examination of its effects on Waldo. In both objectives she holds fast to Schopenhauer's "philosophic truth" of the meaning of life, summarized by

Schreiner as "a striving, and a striving, and an ending in nothing" (*African Farm* 116).

As with any Bildungsroman, the beginning is innocence—and ignorance, an inseparable pair. "In our early youth," Schopenhauer stated, "we sit before life that lies ahead of us like children sitting before the curtain in a theatre, in happy and tense anticipation of whatever is going to appear" (*Essays* 47). This blissful stage of Waldo's existence is brief, and he remembers it in fragments of mental pictures: being carried and cuddled, watching pigs at play, smelling fresh oranges for the first time, feeling the fall of raindrops. Still, amidst even these earliest of memories "a feeling of longing comes over us, —unutterable longing, we cannot tell for what" (153). In adolescence, Waldo discovers "self" and is frightened and puzzled by his own weakness and mortality. Trying to find a friend to calm his fears, he turns to God, both the wrathful God of the Old Testament and one of his own creation, more loving and forgiving. He turns away from the physical world he had loved at face value as a child ("What are flowers to us? They are fuel for the great burning" [156]), adopting a Carlylean attitude towards nature: "Do they not understand that the material world is but a film, through which God's awful spirit-world is shining through on us?" (158).

The time arrives, however, when the world's will becomes incomprehensible and Waldo can no longer find a God to define it for him. He experiences a period of complete loss, a loss of his "place" on God's earth ("Truly we love not the world, neither things that are in it" [161]); he also experiences a spiritual loss:

> Now we have no God. We have had two,—the old God that our fathers handed down to us, that we hated, and never liked; the new one that we made for ourselves, that we loved; but now He has flitted away from us, and we see what He was made of—the shadow of our highest ideal, crowned and throned. Now we have no God. (168)

According to Schopenhauer, the loss of any illusion, whether it be the illusion of ego, free will, or God, is a critical step towards acceptance and a surrender to the will of the world, a state commonly referred to now as "Schopenhauerian pessimism." It is a gradual process for Waldo, and a painful one: "When a soul breaks free from the arms of superstition, bits of the claws and talons break themselves off in him. It is not the work of a day to squeeze them out" (*African Farm* 169). What follows in Waldo's process of disillusionment is an uncanny approximation of Schopenhauer's state of acceptance/pessimism, a final awakening: "And now life takes us up between her finger and thumb, shakes us furiously, till our poor nodding head is well-nigh rolled from our shoulders, and she sets us down a little hardly on the bare earth, bruised and sore, but preternaturally wide awake" (167). Entrance into this state requires three criteria: 1) a realization of man's impotence in the world and his position as victim of the will; 2) an awareness of the world's meaninglessness and complete absence of order; and 3) a knowledge that life is suffering and there is no end to it. Waldo eventually fulfills all three criteria.

When he opens his eyes to the world, unclouded by the deceptive god-mist, he sees that all living things are victims of the world and

> there is no justice. The ox dies in the yoke, beneath its master's whip; it turns its anguished eyes on the sunlight, but there is no sign of recompense to be made it. The black man is shot like a dog, and it goes well with the shooter. The innocent are accused, and the accuser triumphs. If you will take the trouble to scratch the surface anywhere, you will see under the skin a sentient being writhing in impotent anguish. (168-69)

Harder still for Waldo is the purposelessness of this anguish, the randomness of pain and misfortune, the blindness and chaos of the will: "'There is no order, all things are driven about by blind chance. . . .' And so, for us, the human-like driver and guide being gone, all existence, as we look out at it with our chilled, wondering eyes, is an aimless rise and swell of shifting water" (169). Waldo watches a beetle "at work trying to roll home a great ball of dung it had been collecting all morning." Waldo's dog destroys the ball and eats the beetle's legs and head. "And it was all play, and no one could tell what it had lived and worked for. A striving, and a striving, and an ending in nothing" (116).

Looking for a source of life's pain within this chaos is pointless, Schopenhauer stated, because "suffering is essential to life, and therefore does not flow in upon us from outside, but... everyone carries around within himself its perennial source" (*WWR* I, 318). Waldo's awareness of the will, then, must continue until his consciousness is no more. But once the search for the panacea is over, once the searcher realizes the hopelessness of this or any other quest, he can discover in the resulting melancholy or pessimism a kind of peace, an acceptance: "This is in consequence a worthier phenomenon than the constant hunting for ever different deceptive forms" (*WWR* I, 319). The searcher gains not only the release from all pointless endeavors with this acceptance but also a heightened awareness of oneness with all things which strive and fail within the chaotic arena of the will. As George Eliot's *Daniel Deronda* illustrates, Schopenhauerian morality follows from such an awareness in the forms of charity, compassion, and generosity for all things. The most perfect form of charity is asceticism, a total denial of the will to live, a refusal to follow the impulses to survive, a rejection of the urge to procreate and thus add to the suffering of the world and the perpetuation of the will. Few conquer the will in this manner, but Schopenhauer allowed for varying degrees in this starvation of the will.

As Waldo enters into this stage of pessimism, he is neither elated nor devastated. He finds himself in a withdrawn state, life being a matter of indifference to him: "We are not miserable.... We do not wish to live, and we do not wish to die.... In truth, nothing matters" (168, 170). He is aware only of his new perspective of nature and his connection to it. From this, as Schopenhauer illustrated, Waldo rediscovers himself and his world:

> The rocks have been to us a blur of brown; we bend over them, and the disorganized masses dissolve into a many-colored, many shaped, carefully-arranged form of existence. . . . The flat plain has been to us of reach of monotonous red. We look at it, and every handful of sand starts into life. That wonderful people, the ants, we learn to know; see them make war and peace, play and work. . . .

Waldo finds a dead gander and cuts it open, examining the delicate beauty of its blood vessels:

> This we also remark: Of that same exact shape and outline is our thorn-tree seen against the sky in mid-winter; of that shape also is delicate metallic tracery between our rocks. . . . Are they not all the fine branches of one trunk, whose sap flows through us all?
> . . . a living thing, a One. . . . The life that throbs in us is a pulsation from it,—too mighty for our comprehension, not too small.
> (172-75)

He sees in the life cycle of the smallest entity a microcosm of all living development: "Whosoever should portray truly the life and death of a little flower—its birth, sucking in of nourishment, reproduction of its kind, withering and vanishing—would have shaped a symbol of all existence" (196). Waldo discovers that the one sense of order within the chaos of the will is our common bond with all subjects and objects of the "One" will. Once man understands this unity, Schopenhauer wrote,

> he will recognize that same will not only in those phenomena that are quite similar to his own, in men and animals, as their innermost nature, but continued reflection will lead him to recognize the force that shoots and vegetates in the plant, indeed the force by which the crystal is formed, the force that turns the magnet to the North Pole, the force whose shock he encounters from the contact of

metals of different kinds. . ., all these he will recognize as different only in the phenomenon, but the same according to their inner nature. (*WWR* I, 110)

In addition to his feeling of unity with nature, Waldo finds another form of escape from the will in music, another striking affinity between Schopenhauer and Schreiner. Waldo tells his cousin Lyndall: "they made heaven right when they made it all music. It takes you away, away, till you have the things you longed for; you are up close to them. You have got out into a large, free, open place" (319). Music objectifies the will more perfectly than any other experience. Music, Schopenhauer wrote, "is the most powerful of all the arts . . . [because it] expresses the stirrings of the will itself" (*WWR* II, 448-49). Used as a form of escape from the will, music is a consistently recurring theme in novels by women. After all, music, even more than nature (which requires some freedom of movement) was conveniently available to women and a "legal drug" for the treatment of much of their inner turmoil.

With only these two weapons to fight his angst, Waldo's development ends. His presence lingers throughout the last part of the novel, but Schreiner now turns her attention to the subject that will occupy the rest of her literary career: the nature of the will in women. Her study reveals what other works by women in the past have shown: without understanding how women experience individual and cosmic will, Schopenhauer cheated himself out of a convincing source of illumination and verification of his theories. At the center of this study is the belief that woman's will strives, suffers, and endures in a fashion different from men. Schopenhauer appears to have remained entirely ignorant of that force. Fortunately, his literary daughters—unclaimed though they may be—found their own way of showing how the will functions within the "mighty pulsation" of life.

The character of Lyndall, Waldo's cousin, earned Schreiner an important and legitimate place in the burgeoning women's movement at the turn of the century. Largely an autobiographical representation of Schreiner's own awakening to womanhood, Lyndall is a lovely, brilliant, but defeated character, and her story is tragically simple. Lyndall spent her childhood with Waldo growing up on the African farm. She leaves to be educated at a finishing school, hoping to become a productive member of society and find a vent for all of her intellectual abilities. She returns to the farm bitter and disillusioned. She tells Waldo:

> I have discovered that of all the cursed places under the sun, where the hungrier soul can hardly pick up a few grains of knowledge, a girls' boarding-school is the worst. They are called Finishing-schools, and the name tells accurately what they are. They finish everything but imbecility and weakness, and that they cultivate. They are nicely adapted machines for experimenting on the question, "Into how little space can a human soul be crushed?" (218-19)

The finishing school did not completely defeat Lyndall's spirit, however. When she becomes pregnant, she refuses to marry the father, though she loves him, because of the power his love would have over her. Lyndall dies after giving birth to the child who also dies two days later.

Much earlier than Waldo, Lyndall realizes the pain of constant desire and unfulfilled dreams, but unlike Waldo, she suffers from being what she was—a woman in a society which not only thwarts her will but generally denies that she possesses a will at all. Within this framework, a beautiful, intelligent woman who craves more than a life of flowered hats and afternoon teas is doomed to a struggle unknown to her male counterparts. Lyndall attempts to explain her plight to Waldo in a series of passages which are among the most poignant ever written about a woman's inner and outer turmoil:

> "It is not what is done to us, but what is made of us . . . that wrongs us. No man can be really injured but by what modifies himself. . . the world tells us what we are to be. . . . To you [men], it says, Work! And to us it says, Seem! . . . Look at this little chin of mine,

> Waldo, with the dimple in it. . . . though I had a knowledge of all things under the sun, and the wisdom to use it, . . . it would not stead me through life like this little chin. I can win money with it, I can win love; I can win power with it. . . . I once heard an old man say that he never saw intellect help a woman so much as a pretty ankle; and it was the truth. . . . When we ask to be doctors, lawyers, lawmakers, anything but ill-paid drudges, they say, 'No, but you have men's chivalrous attention; now think of that and be satisfied'." (222-23, 225)

Like Waldo, Lyndall is past the point of overt struggling and has entered a stage of pessimistic acceptance. She learned very young that satisfaction was not to be found in this world and that a woman's striving is particularly futile:

> "I am never miserable, and never happy. . . . A little bitterness, a little longing when we are young, a little futile searching for work, a little passionate striving for room for the exercise of our powers,—and then we go with the drove. A woman must march with her regiment. In the end she must be trodden down or go with it; and if she is wise she goes." (219, 224)

This incredible prison was not a foreign place to Schreiner, and in the character of Lyndall she gave voice to many of her own frustrations. She, too, when young wanted to be more than the proper white English girl on an African planation; she wanted to learn and travel. But as Berkman points out, "as a woman she was denied the pulpit instrumental to her missionary father; and the politicians' podium exercised by her brother" (1). Schreiner dreamed all her life of being a doctor, but she knew very well the cruelty of the world towards an intelligent woman. In a letter to Ellis, Schreiner wrote the following bold parable:

> Once God Almighty said: "I will produce a self-working . . . machine for enduring suffering, . . . capable of the largest amount of suffering in a given space," and he made woman. But he wasn't

> satisfied that he reached the highest point of perfection; so he made a man of genius . . .[not] satisfied yet . . . he combined the two—and made a woman of genius—and then he was satisfied!
>
> (*Letters* 146)

Recognizing in herself one of those suffering machines of genius, Schreiner considered the few options available to her: madness? rebellion? writing? Though as Gilbert and Gubar have pointed out in *Madwoman in the Attic,* insanity was not an uncommon avenue of escape for gifted women, "Schreiner had discovered, as had other women of the Victorian era, the emotional release and power of writing. . . . She resorted to the pen, and into her writing she poured her deepest convictions, her most painful experiences, her passion for a better world" (Berkman 1). Writing, then, was Schreiner's act of rebellion. And the battle cry for human rights and female emancipation she began in *African Farm* resounded through her last, unfinished novel, published posthumously in 1926, *From Man to Man.*

Despite its misleading title, one of several titles Schreiner considered for the book, *From Man to Man* is a story of two sisters, Rebekah and Bertie. Rebekah is clearly the voice of Schreiner herself, and her function in the novel is to show what happens to an intelligent woman trapped in an unhappy marriage. Rebekah's husband Frank is a typical soap opera villain, a man who uses marriage as a respectable smoke screen by which to hide his deceptive, lustful activities. Yet Rebekah loves him, and most of her story is an effort to explain to the reader what it is like to be imprisoned both by one's love for another and by societal restraints. Bertie is even more pathetic: as a young girl she gave away her virginity to her schoolmaster, and this youthful, innocent act ruins her for life. She is prohibited from the company of "nice girls" and gentleman, and she is shunned in "good homes." She ends by prostituting herself to rich, older men for survival. These two narrative threads, if they can be called threads, form the plot of *From Man to Man.*

As a novel, it is generally regarded as a failure. Schreiner's style is laboriously didactic and long-winded. The characters are feeble and often embarrassing. Though many critics point to the possibility that Schreiner might have made something of the book had she finished it, there is no real indication that prolonging the plot would have made the already tedious storyline of wronged womanhood a real novel. Though it fails as a novel, it has sustaining cultural and historical value as a feminist tract and would have garnered more authority and respectability if it were in the same format as Schreiner's highly regarded non-fictional study of women, education, and professions, *Women and Labour* (1911). It is as a feminist tract that I wish to discuss *From Man to Man*. The very elements which weaken *From Man to Man* as a novel—the long, intrusive chapters on feminism, aesthetics, religion, and sex—are the only parts of the book worth reading, not for the way in which they further the plot (they do not), but for the discursive manner in which they communicate political/feminist messages.

These chapters also reflect a more sophisticated understanding of Schopenhauer's philosophy of the will. Specifically, Schreiner, in the voice of the unfortunate Rebekah who steals moments away from her miserable marriage to philosophize alone in her private library, explicates rather specific Schopenhauerian ideas about art, unity in nature, and moral compassion. All of these themes are firmly grounded in the understanding of the will and its role in women's lives. *From Man to Man* suggests, therefore, the distinct possibility that Schreiner had spent a great deal of time analyzing Schopenhauer's ideas, integrating his thoughts with others who had impressed her (principally Emerson and Herbert Spencer) and coming up with her own theories of aesthetics and human purpose. The degree to which she echoes Schopenhauer is startling, and the unique treatment of the will in relation to women's lives is, finally, horrifying.

Schreiner viewed the writing of *From Man to Man* as a kind of Schopenhauerian immersion in art which not only allowed for her own temporary escape from physical ills and social frustrations but also as an act of compassion to the pain of others, the most moral of all acts according to Schopenhauer. The title itself reflects Schreiner's altruistic purpose. Her husband explained in his introduction to the novel, "The title is taken from a sentence of John (later Lord) Morley's, which runs as follows, except that I have forgotten the adjective: 'From man to man nothing matters but . . . charity.' The missing word connotes 'boundless,' 'all-embracing,' or some such large and generous attitude of the mind" (*From Man to Man* ix). In a letter to Ellis dated 12 July 1884, Schreiner wrote:

> You know, all these months when I have been in such suffering, and have had that yearning to do something for others that I feel when I am in pain, I have always built upon the fact that *From Man to Man* will help other people, for it will help to make men more tender to women, because they will understand them better; it will make some women more tender to others; it will comfort some women by showing them that others have felt as they do. (*Letters* 28)

Her compassion for others and her need to ease their pain was a direct result of her own physical and emotional suffering and her intense desire for escape. She was tortured by asthma and heart disease, and she was constantly troubled by the restraints placed on her as a writer and professional because of her gender. Writing was her escape, her attempt to objectify her pain: "Writing makes me happy because then my own little miserable life is *not*" (*Letters* 50). Here Schreiner expresses a fundamental of Schopenhauer's philosophy: happiness is impossible without a denial of the will, a turning away from the life force. The artist, by concentrating on objectifying the Idea (the thing-in-itself), temporarily achieves peace. Schopenhauer explains:

> When . . . an external cause or inward disposition suddenly raises us out of the endless stream of willing and snatches knowledge from the thraldom of the will, the attention is now no longer

> directed to the motives of willing, but comprehends things free from their relation to the will. . . . Then all at once the peace, always sought but always escaping us . . . comes to us of its own accord. (*WWR* I, 196)

Whether it be through art or pure asceticism, then, the need to *be* must be overcome before peace can be attained.

Unfortunately for Schreiner, the very means by which she could temporarily escape from the will—her writing—became itself a strong assertion of the will and a source of endless striving. Her writing formed a determined expression of her need to exist. Much as a mother strives to survive the pain of childbirth in order to perpetuate life, both her own and the new life, Schreiner as an artist struggled to survive, literally, long enough to complete the expression of her will, thus assuring its continuation. The need to give birth to *From Man to Man* became an obsession, a manifestation rather than a denial of the will. She wrote her husband in 1907, "Oh, I wish I could get my book done before I die. It may not be any good; but I feel I have to do it. I used to feel I couldn't die till it was done, that fate wouldn't let it be. Now I know that anything may be; you trust and hope for years, but things never come" (*Letters* 268-69). Even at the very end of her life, faced with the probability that death would cheat her of sufficient time to finish her work, Schreiner gives testimony to one of the most important reasons for the need for art and our instinct to create, according to Schopenhauer: sympathy for the human family. Shortly before her death she told a friend, "It isn't the pain and weakness one minds, it's the not being able to work. My one novel especially I would have liked so to finish. I feel that if only one lonely and struggling woman read it and found strength and comfort from it one would not feel one had lived quite in vain" (*Letters* 321-22). Schreiner knew that the artist can function as the great healer, and by creating a work of sympathy and beauty she might be a part of the highest form of altruism, according to Schopenhauer: "The world as representation [in art] . . ., by tearing ourselves from willing and letting it alone take possession of our consciousness, is the most delightful, and the only innocent, side of life. We have to regard art as the greater enhancement, the more perfect development, of all this. . . . It may be called the flower of life" (*WWR* I, 266). Art, then, is a way of exhibiting compassion for one's fellow beings while simultaneously attempting to objectify the will; the artist, that is, is the instrument of the force of the will which constantly attempts to assert itself in all things. Schreiner paraphrases Schopenhauer's view of creation in *From Man to Man*:

> Everywhere this binding moving creative force moves at the very heart of things, growing more and more important and complex as creatures mount in the scale of life, till it reaches its apotheosis in the artist, in whom the desire to create dominates all else, who, not from himself but by the necessity of some force within himself, is spent and must spend himself to produce that which gives infinite joy without ever being used up, over which there need be no struggle. (189)

Again like Schopenhauer, Schreiner saw the artistic impulse as a sophisticated extension of "the mysterious instinct to create and reproduce . . . the fundamental power manifested in all we call life" (190).

But as the history of writers and writing makes all too clear, when this power manifests itself in a female artist, it is often denied, starved, or misdirected, and can subsequently lead to a tragic, painful waste of positive potential. Long before Virginia Woolf hypothesized the achievements of a female Shakespeare, Schreiner entertained a similar thought in *From Man to Man*, grieving for the centuries of creative female impulses channeled in traditional, unfulfilling directions:

> We have a Shakespeare; but what of the possible Shakespeares we might have had, who passed their life from youth upward brewing currant wine and making pastries for fat country squires to eat,

> with no glimpse of the freedom of life and actions, . . .stifled out without one line written, simply because, being of the weaker sex, life gave no room for action and grasp on life? (195)

Because the need to create is one of the most powerful assertions of the will, this kind of suppression, either individual or collective, leads only to intensified corruption, illness, or misplaced activity, according to Schopenhauer: "All <u>willing</u> springs from lack, from deficiency, and thus from suffering" (*WWR* I, 196) or, in Schreiner's words, "No state will ever be final; as soon as we have attained to it we shall cease to need it" (*Letters* 75-76). Since any permanent suppression of the will is impossible, any effort to do so will result in some kind of deviation: "We see striving everywhere impeded in many ways, everywhere struggling and fighting, and hence always as suffering. Thus that there is no ultimate aim of striving means that there is no measure or end of suffering" (*WWR* I, 309). Of course, what women writers like Schreiner understood through experience, Schopenhauer completely overlooked in his philosophy: the world-wide suppression of the creative, intellectual energies of women would cause intensified pain and suffering in the world and prevent access to a fountain of compassion which Schopenhauer insisted was necessary for survival. If willing stems from a lack and suffering is its result, then unfulfilled desires can only contribute to the world's pain. Schreiner stated the problem clearly, with evident irony: the stereotypical "weakness" of women and minority races was a direct result of their suppression, and the world would continue to be a colder and darker place than it could be until these people were freed from societal restraints. According to Berkman, "The insidious effects of thwarted female energies, Schreiner saw, crippled men and children as much as women themselves" (32). Looking at the supposedly great civilization of the Greeks, the character of Rebekah in *From Man to Man* observes: "What was that much vaunted culture but a delicate iridescent film overlying the seething mass of servile agricultural and domestic slaves and of women, nominally of the dominant class, but hardly less servile and perhaps ignorant, who constituted the bulk of its inhabitants?" (164). Such a world, Schreiner contended, had to fail:

> It would be as rational to expect that such a form of culture, brought into existence for a moment by a combination of happy conditions, could hand itself down from generation to generation, expanding and strengthening as it grew, as to expect a spray of shrub, plucked and placed in a vase of water in a hothouse, though it might bloom profusely for a few days, should permanently propagate itself and persistently grow when it was without ground and had no root. (164)

But this analogy is not entirely apt. Most women, including Rebekah and Bertie, have far too many roots and far too much earth to ground them: the problem is finding room to stretch and grow. In *From Man to Man*, Schreiner addresses the social taboo of female artistry and the sense that women had to hide their "shameful" desires to grow and create. In the preface to the novel, Rebekah talks to an imaginary female child: "If I tell you a secret, you mustn't tell anyone else! I'm a person that makes up stories! I write books! . . . If you like to make up stories, I shall never let anyone laugh at you, when you walk up and down and talk to yourself. I know you must!" (22-23). The hidden desire festers and, as with any plant being strangled by its own roots, disease sets in. With Schreiner's women the disease takes the form of spiritual hunger and eventual physical and emotional atrophy.

Schreiner's intelligent, resourceful female characters realize very young that they are hungry. Both the source of and satisfaction for this hunger are unknown, but its constant presence is certain. At the beginning of *From Man to Man*, Rebekah has decided to leave the home of her childhood and her beloved sister, Bertie, to marry her cousin Frank. Like Lyndall in *African Farm*, Rebekah is both intelligent (her interest in plant and animal life would have suited her for a career in botany) and self-aware; therefore she reflects on the process in which she is now engaged and wonders:

> What was she leaving for? . . . There was—well—a vague, insatiable hunger? Books, black beetles, well-performed duties—she had tried them all, and she was dying of hunger. . . . Was it a voice from that primal depth of nature which, before man was man, called beast to beast and kind to kind? . . . An ox at the roadside, when it is dying of hunger and thirst, does not lie down—up and down, seeking it knows not what; —but it does not lie down. (56-57)

Schopenhauer would respond that humankind will sooner struggle, wander, fight, and suffer than simply rest or surrender; the denial of the will is much more difficult than its assertion, even though achievement of the former will bring peace and continuation of the latter only perpetual suffering, as Rebekah's life illustrates.[2]

Her marriage fails, owing mainly to her husband's constant infidelities, which Rebekah dutifully tries to dismiss as a part of his manly nature.[3] Her attempts to steal moments of enlightenment in her own little library cease to satisfy; she is doomed to a life of emptiness and frustration. When Rebekah finally realizes that there is no hope for change in her life or her marriage, she is momentarily overwhelmed by the temptation and release of suicide: "Something rose and surged through her; from her feet it seemed to mount till it reached to her brain and swept all before it. She would go into the house and gather them all in her arms, those children born of lust and falsehood, and they and she and the unborn would pass away together!" (277). The outcome of Rebekah's flirtation with suicide suggests that Schreiner likely was knowledgeable of Schopenhauer's discussion of the allure of suicide for the suffering person; she also recognized Schopenhauer's insistence upon the futility of suicide as a means of quieting the will. The will to live, even under unbearable conditions, is greater than the desire to die in the healthy individual. Those who commit suicide, instead of denying the will to live, actually affirm its hold over them and only succeed in perpetuating the life force through eternity. "Far from being a denial of the will, " Schopenhauer states,

> Suicide is a phenomenon of the will's strong affirmation.... The suicide denies merely the individual, not the species.... since life is always certain to the will-to-live, and suffering is essential to life, suicide ... is a quite futile and foolish act, for the thing-in-itself remains unaffected by it. (*WWR* I 398-99)

Rebekah identifies her life force by name in the brief battle between her will to survive and her need to end the suffering: "For an instant the impulse seemed to gain upon her with fearful force. Then slowly *her will* [emphasis mine] took command again and she annihilated it [the desire to die]" (277).

Though Schopenhauer asserted that suicide is no escape from the will, he did not provide for the case of a woman whose will to live saves her from physical death but whose love of life has diminished to the point of spiritual death. Schopenhauer regarded a turning away from life as desirable asceticism, but Rebekah neither removes herself from the world (she continues throughout the remainder of the novel to care for her children and herself) nor does she partake in life (her soul, never truly her own, died by the hands of her husband, who owned it). Schreiner sees Rebekah's form of existence as a common situation for people who are denied the power to control their own lives.

It is also in *From Man to Man* that Schreiner wholeheartedly embraces the Schopenhauerian world view and rejects traditional Christian ideology. Seeing the universe as "a whole" rather than "a thing of shreds and patches and unconnected parts" at the mercy of the "great individual Will" (155), Schreiner endorses Schopenhauer's belief (as well as that of many others, Emerson in particular) that man is the life force in microcosm, an idea she entertained in *African Farm* and developed more fully in *From Man to Man*. In the central chapter in the latter, "Raindrops in the Avenue," Rebekah muses:

> Between spirit that beats within me and body through which it acts, between mind and matter, between man and beast and plant and

> plant and earth, between life that has been the life it is, I am able to see nowhere a sharp line of severance, but a great, pulsating, always interacting whole. So that at last it comes to be, that, when I hear my own heart beat, I actually hear in it nothing but one throb in that life which has been and is—in which we live and move and have our being and are constantly sustained. (153)

For Schreiner, then, "an *extraneous* [emphasis mine] will dealing arbitrarily with the things of existence was inconceivable" (156); the will was the essence of all existence, a part of it, not a ruling force outside of it. Inherent in this belief is the need for a community of all things and a sense of social and moral responsibility for each other. It is this political, philosophical, and moral stance, along with her clear pleas for women's rights, which form her legacy and echo throughout the writing of generations of female artists to come.

Chapter Three
Virginia Woolf, Bloomsbury Aesthetics, and Schopenhauer

In September of 1917, Virginia Woolf read an article by Viscount Harberton (Ernest Arthur George Pomeroy) in the *Times Literary Supplement* (Woolf, *Essays* 157). In this article, Harberton criticizes the reading habits of his day, contending that people are reading too much and ignoring their own common sense. In the course of his argument, Harberton endorses the reading of Schopenhauer, however, and uses several excerpts from the German philosopher's works as epigraphs. Woolf responded to Harberton's argument in a satiric essay, "To Read or Not to Read":

> Such is the bustle and sprightliness of Lord Harberton's mind, such the audacity with which he flies from tariff Reform to inoculation, from Party Government to Home Rule, to settle finally upon the flanks of the incorrigible reader, that we were just laying a faggot to our bookcase in the hope of catching his style, when we came upon the names of Schopenhauer and Herbert Spencer. No praise is too high for them; in their books, we are told, we shall find the secret of the universe. After all, then, Lord Harberton is merely one of those cultivated people who play the innocent for a holiday. Still, one reader will give him the benefit of the doubt and take his advice to the extent of refraining for ever from the pages of Schopenhauer. (*Essays* 157)

No evidence exists to suggest that Woolf broke her word. In all likelihood, she never read Schopenhauer. But she knew of him and his works. Through George Moore, Schopenhauer's ideas on art and will became a cornerstone of Bloomsbury aesthetics, and among Woolf's Bloomsbury friends, Schopenhauer became a major subject of conversation (Levy 175). Leonard Woolf, Roger Fry, E.M. Forster, all read Schopenhauer (Leonard Woolf, in fact, was one of the first philosophical critics of his day to address Schopenhauer in his publications) and debated his philosophy and its relevance to their work. Never far from these philosophical conversations, or from Leonard's work (though she occasionally feigned boredom), Woolf absorbed and evaluated the philosophical contributions of Schopenhauer. Eventually, they would make a strong statement in her own work.

According to Patrick Bridgewater, author of *George Moore and German Pessimism*, Moore found in Schopenhauer an answer to what he considered Hegel's inane idealism, as well as a foundation for his own aesthetic theory. Moore was probably first introduced to the works of Schopenhauer during his visits to Paris in the 1870's and 1880's, a time in which Schopenhauer enjoyed considerable fame in France. Moore's acquaintances from this period, including William Butler Yeats, contributed to his enthusiasm for the German philosopher's anti-Hegelian, anti-historicism, anti-world philosophy (Bridgewater 27).[1] Echoing Schopenhauer's disdain for Hegel, Moore stated in *Philosophical Studies*, "Hegel's main service to philosophy has consisted in giving a name to and erecting into principle, a type of fallacy to which experience had shown philosophers, along with the rest of mankind, to be addicted" (16). Moore's later writing specifically acknowledges a great debt to Schopenhauer. The Schopenhauerian perspective on the world as representation of the will, as a product of man's creation, appealed both to Moore's egoism as well as his insistence on art as the objectification of man's desires. As Bridgewater notes, Moore hungered for a philosophy which would satisfy his great enthusiasm for life while grounding his pessimistic tendencies, and the diet he needed in 1888 evidently included Schopenhauer's emphasis on the blindness of the Will, on the role of chance in life, and the primacy of instinct and the irrational intellect. . . . No doubt the idea that he, George Moore, was the world, also appealed to him. (35)

But it is Schopenhauer's influence on Moore's aesthetic theory which is most significant as Bloomsbury's inheritance. Moore uses Schopenhauer to explain, for example, the relationship between idea and symbol, the symbol being the tool by which the artist represents the idea drawn out of the thing itself. As Bridgewater concludes from this passage, "What Moore had in mind was almost certainly Schopenhauer's view of music" (16). Moore was attracted by a theory which empowers art to the extent Schopenhauer's does, to the level of a panacea for the tormenting will. Moore's famous ethical discussion of "the Ideal" also reflects a Schopenhauerian awareness of art as beauty and communal interaction as one way of minimizing the ugliness of the world. The spiritual power of art as man's salvation and a primary source of good becomes a cornerstone of Bloomsbury aesthetics and a central focus of Virginia Woolf's great novel of the tension between art and chaos, *To the Lighthouse*.

Any question regarding the extent to which the ideas of George Moore actually influenced the various members of Bloomsbury is answered by Leon Edel who represents a common consensus of opinion when he asserts that Leonard Woolf, Roger Fry, and Clive Bell "were apostles in a special sense of that word and G.E. Moore was their Christ; he gave them their religion" (53). This religion of aesthetics and human relations led Moore's apostles to many Schopenhauerian conclusions about the role of art in the affairs of man as well as the essence of art itself. A look at the aesthetic commentaries by Fry and Bell in particular reveals an unmistakable kinship with Schopenhauer and an influence never before acknowledged by Bloomsbury critics.

Both Fry and Bell write about "significant form" in art, maintaining that it is this characteristic which gives art its power. In *Vision and Design*, Fry identifies a work of art which possesses significant form as "the outcome of an endeavor to express an idea rather than to create a pleasing object" (236). After identifying this significant form as "essential reality," Bell adds, "Call it what you will, the thing that I am talking about is that which lies behind the appearance of all things—that which gives to all things their individual significance, the thing in itself, the ultimate reality" (*Art* 54). Of course, Schopenhauer calls this "thing," this "Idea," the objectification of the will, and he is in complete accord with Bell and Fry in his assessment of its power:

> What kind of knowledge is it that considers what continues to exist outside and independently of all relations, but which alone is really essential to the world, the true content of its phenomena, that which is subject to no change, and is therefore with equal truth for all time, in a word, the Ideas that are the immediate and adequate objectivity of the thing-in-itself, of the will? It is art, the work of genius. It repeats the eternal Ideas apprehended through pure contemplation, the essential and abiding element in all the phenomena of the world. (*WWR* I, 184).

Just as Bell recognizes in art the power to "transport us to that remote aesthetic beatitude in which [we are] *freed from humanity* [emphasis mine]" (110), Schopenhauer also observes that aesthetic enjoyment allows for "the bliss and peace of mind of pure knowledge free from all willing, and thus from all individuality and the pain that results therefrom" (*WWR* I, 212). Fry further illustrates this point in his discussion of the experience of viewing Cezanne's painting. The observer is

> held in a kind of thrilled suspense by the unsuspected correspondences of all related elements. . . . the more one looks the more do these dispersed indications begin to play together, to compose rhythmic phrases which articulate the apparent confusion,

> till at last all seems to come together to the eye into an austere and impressive architectural construction, which is all the more moving in that it emerges from this apparent chaos. (*Cezanne* 70)

It is this harmony (in this case in painting, but it exists as clearly in music, architecture, poetry, and so on) which permits temporary escape from the will. Schopenhauer identifies the beauty of painting as "the mere harmony of colours, the agreeable aspect of the grouping, the favorable distribution of light and shade, and the tone. . . .[This] beauty promotes the condition of pure knowing" (*WWR* I, 422). Bell concludes *Art* with a passage which could easily have come from Schopenhauer's work:

> He who goes daily into the world of aesthetic emotion returns to the world of human affairs equipped to face it courageously and even a little contemptuously. And if by comparison with aesthetic rapture he finds most human passion trivial, he need not on that account become unsympathetic or inhuman. For practical purposes, even, it is possible that the religion of art will serve a man better than the religion of humanity. He may learn in another world to doubt the extreme importance of this, but if that doubt dims his enthusiasm for some things that are truly excellent it will dispel his illusions about many that are not. (190)

Art, then, to Bloomsbury and Schopenhauer, represented a great force of salvation and escape from the malevolent world will, a means of bringing order to external chaos and peace to internal torment, if only for the "sublime" moment.

In her most aesthetic novel, Virginia Woolf attempts to come to terms with the expectations for art and the artist in a chaotic, haunted world. *To the Lighthouse* is a novel about creation and destruction. Often compared to a Monet painting, the novel plays with the light, shadows, and colors of passing time, always placing art at the very core of existence, testing its endurance and relevance.[2] To observe that Woolf employs the artistic theories of her

Bloomsbury counterparts throughout the novel is no surprise: Fry was one of Woolf's most respected critics and literary advisors. As Panthea Reid observes in her 1996 study of Woolf's life and aesthetics, "*To the Lighthouse* explicitly illustrates, embodies, and discusses Roger's aesthetic theories" (303). According to David Dowling in *Bloomsbury Aesthetics and the Novels of Forster and Woolf*, Woolf wanted to dedicate *To the Lighthouse* to Fry in recognition of his keeping her "on the right path, so far as writing goes, more than anyone." Dowling also contends that Woolf was "well-informed" of aesthetic theory (97). She read Bells's *Art* in 1914 and wrote in a letter to him, "I like the chapters of theory more than the historical chapters" (*Letters* II, 46). Exactly how Woolf works with aesthetic theory in *To the Lighthouse* has been widely discussed. But if Bloomsbury aesthetics can be seen as a fair representation of much of Schopenhauer's theories on art, the meaning of Woolf's aesthetic message, including all of its tones, colors, and movement, requires another look. A Schopenhauerian perspective of Woolf's word-picture will reveal much darker and much more ominous hues than critics to date have noticed.

Before meeting the artist Lily Briscoe in *To the Lighthouse*, the reader's eyes are arrested by the landscape created by the "first mover" of this aesthetic universe, Woolf herself. What strikes the reader initially about this landscape is the attention given the environment. The very first sentence places Nature in the role of determining action. Mrs. Ramsey promises her son a trip to the lighthouse "if it's fine tomorrow" (3), and immediately Mr. Ramsey, speaking in the deterministic manner he maintains throughout the novel, announces that in fact "it won't be fine tomorrow" (4). The role of Nature in the novel is never diminished; it takes the form of a living, malevolent character, consistently greedy, unpredictable, and oppressive: "With equal complacence she saw [mankind's] misery, his meanness, and his torture" (134). The wind blows "from the worst possible direction for landing at the Lighthouse" (5); the night air breathes with a "perfectly indifferent chill" (115-16); "the torment of storms" represents "gigantic chaos streaked with lightning ... pierced by no light of reason" resembling "idiot games, ... as if the universe were battling and tumbling, in brute confusion and wanton lust aimlessly by itself" (134, 135).

The seasons, instead of possessing their own beauty and value, are merely a sequence of desolation and violence: "the autumn leaves, ravaged as they are, take on the flash of tattered flags, kindling in the gloom of cool cathedral caves where gold letters on the marble pages describe death in battle and how bones bleach and burn far away in Indian sands" (127). As winter approaches, the nights "are full of wind and destruction; the trees plunge and bend and their leaves fly helter skelter.... Also the sea tosses itself and breaks itself" (128). Even spring is disdainful of existence, "like a virgin fierce in her chastity, scornful in her purity ... entirely careless" (131), and its flowers "looking before them, looking up, yet beholding nothing, [are] eyeless, and so terrible" (135); and summer, perhaps the cruelest of all for being "the hopeful," making it "impossible to resist the strange intimation .. That good triumphs, happiness prevails, order rules," in fact brings heat, wind, and death. Summer "sent its spies ... weeds that had grown close to the glass in the night tapped methodically at the window-pane" (132). In the summer winds one could hear "ominous sounds like the measured blows of hammers dulled on felt ... glass tinkled in the cupboard as if a giant voice had shrieked so loud in its agony that tumblers stood inside a cupboard vibrated too" (133). And summer takes the lives of Prue and Andrew Ramsey.

In *Virginia Woolf's Major Novels: The Fables of Anon.*, Maria Dibattista recognizes a nihilistic Nature at work in *To the Lighthouse* "expressed in a Schopenhauer vision ... as the pure and wanton will that mocks the human idea of order" (98). It is the relationship between this will, this force, and the people struggling against it that forms the subject of Woolf's novel and the object of Lily Briscoe's painting. As Woolf's word-picture takes shape, the characters gradually acknowledge this force which moves them and all other things, and the way in which they accept this knowledge provides insight into Woolf's aesthetic vision.

As Lily's painting finally objectifies her perceptions, "something which she sees as 'truth'" (Marsh 157), at the close of the novel, she sees the unifying and harmonizing power of art promised by Schopenhauer and preached by Bloomsbury.

Lily is not the first to attempt to bring order to chaos, however; Mrs. Ramsey is herself a valiant soldier against the forces of the will, but she hasn't the appropriate weapons. She attempts to fight Nature with humanity, good will, and denial. Mrs. Ramsey's battles with the will, with the inescapable life-force, exemplify the common human response to entrapment: denial, fear, followed by passive acceptance. This, Schopenhauer recognized, is the process of living, submitting to the yoke of the will. What seemed remarkable to Schopenhauer is that human beings attempt, over and over again, to deny or escape this yoke in the face of irrefutable proof of the will's dominance over them. As we have seen, *To the Lighthouse* is immersed in an atmosphere of destruction and turmoil, a world repeatedly evaluated by the phrase, "someone had blundered" (18). Still, Mrs. Ramsey seeks to deny her apparent environment and insist on order. She tells her distraught son, "Perhaps you will wake up and find the sun shining and the birds singing" (15) while she hears the wind blowing and the waves crashing outside. As she listens, her initial attempts to perceive her world as peaceful and nurturing are gradually destroyed:

> The waves on the beach . . . seemed consolingly to repeat over and over again as she sat with the children the words of some old cradle song, murmured by nature, "I am guarding you—I am your support," but at other times suddenly and unexpectedly . . . had no such kindly meaning, but like a ghostly roll of drums remorselessly beat the measure of life, made one think of the destruction of the island and its engulfment in the sea, and warned her . . And made her look up with an impulse of terror. (15-16)

As Dibattista notes, Mrs. Ramsey's mind "beholds, but cannot transform, the vital chaos it contemplates" (98). Even the fictional worlds she creates reveal the irrational, out of control force she wishes to ignore. The bedtime story she reads to her children is a mirror of both Mrs. Ramsey's external environment and her inner turmoil:

> Outside a great storm was raging and blowing so hard that he could scarcely keep his feet; houses and tress toppled over, the mountains trembled, rocks rolled into the sea, the sky was pitch black, and it thundered and lightened, and the sea came in with black waves as high as church towers and mountains, and all with white foam at the top. (61)

It is this fictional passage which reveals Mrs. Ramsey's actual state of mind: she is, as Mr. Ramsey often observes, a pessimist. Her outward guise of pacification and optimism is simply the feeble weapon she uses to fend off the darkness (she hasn't the powerful tool possessed by Lily—a brush, or Mr. Carmichael—poetic genius, or her husband—disinterested scholarship). Her fragmented thoughts expose an acute awareness of the hopelessness of her struggle "in the presence of her old antagonist, life" (79): her daughter Rose, she knows, "would grow up. . . and would suffer" (81); her son James "will never be so happy again" than in his childhood (58) for he and her other children were fated to "grow up into long-legged monsters" (58); life itself, she believed, was "terrible, hostile, and quick to pounce on you if you gave it a chance. There were the eternal problems: suffering; death; the poor" (60); and she is unquestionably at the mercy of her own longings: "There is something I want—something I have come to get, and she fell deeper and deeper without knowing quite what it was" (119). In perhaps her strongest Schopenhauerian observation, Mrs. Ramsey expresses a foreboding which echoes throughout the novel that the world is an uncontrolled, undisciplined entity whose creation must be the product of something or someone who had indeed "blundered":

> How could any Lord have made this world? she asked. With her mind she had always seized the fact that there is no reason, order, justice: but suffering, death, the poor. There was no treachery too base for the world to commit; she knew that. No happiness lasted; she knew that. (64)

Like all who are ensnared in the world, Mrs. Ramsey struggles in various ways to cope, or even escape for a time. Her methods, given Schopenhauer's philosophy, are predictable. She immerses herself in the lives and concerns of others, in an attempt at a kind of Schopenauerian compassion which might in some way eclipse self: "For her own self-satisfaction was it that she wished so instinctively to help, to give" (41). Her dinner party, the central focus of Part One of the novel, is an example of her attempt to overcome the darkness. The dinner is one of many of Mrs. Ramsey's efforts to bring together the disparate members of the seaside group, all already pathetic victims of life (Mr. Carmichael, though a gifted poet, escapes "the innumerable miseries of his life" [40] through opium addiction; Tansley hides within his scholarship; and Lily immerses herself in art). The dinner party scene is a perfect example of Mrs. Ramsey's battles with the clamorous, discordant forces of life. With an array of human casualties before her at the table, she feels "the whole of the effort of merging and flowing and creating rested on her" (83). If only human relationships, communication, could be satisfactory, one might have a chance against the chaos. But she is soon overwhelmed by the fruitlessness of human contact: she becomes aware "of the pettiness of some part of her, and of human relations, how flawed they are, how despicable, how self-seeking, at their best" (42), and "nothing seemed to have merged. They all sat separate" (83). At one point Lily Briscoe sees in Mrs. Ramsey's desperate glance the following message of pending self-destruction: "Unless you apply some balm to the anguish of this hour and say something nice . . ., life will run upon the rocks—indeed I hear the grating and the growling at this minute" (92).

Feeling like the "beaten mariner" in her book of poems (119), Mrs. Ramsey experiences at this point a Schopenhauerian surrender of will, but it is restored through compassion for Mr. Bankes and his unmarried state:

> In pity for him, life now being strong enough to bear her on again, she began all this business, as a sailor not without weariness sees the wind fill his sail and yet hardly wants to be off again and thinks how, had the ship sunk, he would have whirled round and round and found rest on the floor of the sea. (84)

She overcomes her very natural (and desirable, according to Schopenhauer) longing to cease to exist by focusing outside of herself. Her desire to urge others towards marriage is, she realizes, a way to channel life away from her: "She was driven on, too quickly she knew, almost as if it were as escape for her too, to say that people must marry; people must have children" (60), despite the fact that she knows that this continuation of life is "bearing in its bosom the seeds of death" (100). Mrs. Ramsey is also saved from total despair at the dinner party through a successful and satisfying attempt to remove herself from the world through objects outside of herself, in this case a bowl of fruit which she likens to a still-life work of art:

> Her eyes had been going in and out among the curves and shadows of the fruit, among the rich purples of the lowland grapes, then over the horny ridge of the shell, putting a yellow against a purple, a curved shape against a round shape, without knowing why she did it, or why, every time she did it, she felt more and more serene. (108-109)

Other art forms serve the same purpose. When reading sonnets, "her mind felt swept, felt clean," the poetry offering her "the essence sucked out of life and held rounded here—the sonnet" (121). She finds solace in private contemplation of art and other inanimate objects. Such concentration on the "other" temporarily quiets the longings of the will, according to Schopenhauer, and allows the individual a sense of peace. It also verifies the individual's inextricable bond with all things, since the unity felt with nature or other objects is merely the recognition of the one cause, one source of all things: the will. "It was odd," Mrs. Ramsey observes, "how if one was alone, one leant to inanimate things; trees, streams, flowers; felt they expressed one; felt they became one; felt they knew one, in a sense were one" (63). In this state, a loss of self brings a sense of harmony, much like the aesthetic experience of losing oneself in a work of art:

> Often she found herself sitting and looking, sitting and looking, with her work in her hands until she became the thing she looked at. . . . Losing personality, one lost the fret, the hurry, the stir; and there rose to her lips always some exclamation of triumph over life when things came together in this peace, this rest, this eternity. (63)

Still, Mrs. Ramsey is aware that the only real eternity is the eternal life of the will and its endless movement. Following each of these episodes of brief respite, Mrs. Ramsey announces to herself, "But this cannot last. . . . It could not last" (104, 106). Part One ends with Mrs. Ramsey's acknowledgment of the passing of all things. "Her world was changing," but still she insists that "all must be in order," as the winds continue to blow the leaves and the words of a poem spoken by her husband echo through her mind: "And all the lives we ever lived/And all the lives to be,/Are full of trees and changing leaves" (110).

While Schopenhauerian pessimism pervades *To the Lighthouse*, primarily through the character of Mrs. Ramsey and the presence of nihilistic nature, Woolf also poses a highly sophisticated question to her readers concerning the efficacy of pessimism and optimism. In fact, she provides definitions of the terms which Schopenhauer struggled throughout most of his career to establish. Essentially, through the juxtaposition of Mrs. Ramsey with Mr. Ramsey, a definition of pessimism as a desirable state of mind develops, and the reader is faced with the Schopenhauerian edict to acknowledge the world's suffering and mankind's inescapable role in it: only through this acceptance can peace be found. Though Mr. Ramsey calls his wife a pessimist, his objection to her attitude is that she does not simply accept the struggle of life; rather she always evaluates and questions it. Mrs. Ramsey mistakenly interprets her husband's admonishments to cease her "gloominess" as evidence of his optimism (after all, he tells her "it's wrong to be pessimistic" [123]), but nothing could be further from the truth (70). He is perhaps the darkest, most Schopenhauerian character in the novel. Mr. Ramsey's brand of pessimism is Schopenhauerian in the sense that it creates a certain peace through an acceptance of human beings' pathetic place in the world. Even Mrs. Ramsey remarks, "It was odd . . . that with all his gloom and desperation he was happier, more hopeful on the whole, than she was. . . . How strange it was that being convinced, as he was, of all sorts of horrors, seemed not to depress him but to cheer him" (59, 70). Mrs. Ramsey cannot believe that her husband's acknowledgment of the world's strife can bring him anything but misery, and she dismisses his frequent attempts to inform her of his observations about "the poor, little world": "All this phrase-making was a game, she thought, for if she had said half what he said, she would have blown her brains out by now" (69, 71). But what Mrs. Ramsey fails to understand is that her husband's acceptance of the transitory nature of all things and the absolute meaninglessness of existence releases him from the very struggle she endures. Mr. Ramsey realizes, as he approaches old age, that he will never reach his goals; he might make it to Q, but "he would never reach R" (35). Yet knowing the fallacy of Hegelian progress frees him from any sense of loss or recrimination. After all, mankind is not progressive. Why, then, should he grieve about any failure or lost opportunity? By rejecting Hegel, Mr. Ramsey rejects despair and accepts true Schopenhauerian pessimism: "If Shakespeare had never existed, he asked, would the world have differed much from what it is today? Does the progress of civilisation depend on great men? Is the lot of the average human being better now than in the time of the Pharaohs?" (42-43). Though he is proud of his scholarship (appropriately concerned with "subject and object and the nature of reality" [23]), his disbelief in individual greatness and progress diminishes his ego to the point where he can accept his mortality as well as his ultimate union with the larger life force, an admirable human achievement, according to Schopenhauer. Mr. Ramsey understands that "the very stone one kicks with one's boot will outlast Shakespeare. His own little light would shine, not very brightly, for a year or two, and would then be merged in some bigger light, and that in a bigger still" (35).

Of course, Mr. Ramsey struggles too, as all living things must, and, again as he must, he suffers: "To be caught happy in a world of misery was for an honest man the most despicable of crimes" (44). He also seeks escape, like his wife, through art: reading "fortifies him. He clean forgot all the little rubs and digs of the day, . . . forgot himself completely . . . forgot his own bothers and failures completely" (119-120). And he desires compassion. In fact, Nicholas Marsh suggests that Mr. Ramsey's "demand for sympathy" is a major motivation for Lily's escape into art (156). But Mr. Ramsey's struggle is less with the will itself or his own needs than against the weakness and uncertainty in others to accept their fate "to perish, each alone" (167) and yet endure: "It was his fate . . To stand on this little ledge facing the dark of human ignorance" (44). In many ways he resembles the very essence of will in his undeniable demand to be, to assert his existence. It is this quality his children fear and hate, just as all beings resist the will for possessing similar characteristics:

> He was incapable of untruth; never tampered with a fact; never altered a disagreeable word to suit the pleasure or convenience of any mortal being, least of all his children, who, sprung from his loins, should be aware from childhood that life is difficult; facts uncompromising; and the passage to that fabled land where our brightest hopes are extinguished, our frail barks founder in darkness, . . . one that needs, above all, courage, truth, and the power to endure. (4)

Even on the excursion to the lighthouse as the novel closes, his adolescent daughter and son feel his undeniable power over them and their environment:

> What remained intolerable . . . was that crass blindness and tyranny of his which had poisoned [Cam's] childhood and raised bitter storms, so that even now she woke in the night trembling with rage and remembered some command of his; some insolence; "Do this," "do that," his dominance; his "Submit to me." (170)

The Schopenhauerian language here is evident: like the will itself, Mr. Ramsey is blind and intolerant, forcing one to tremble, rage, and finally submit.

The "object" of Lily Briscoe's final painting is, then, a landscape of disorder and conflicting forces: Mr. Ramsey's wilfulness matched full force by the environment's chaotic flux; Mrs. Ramsey's anguished attempts to represent order within chaos; and Nature's own role as manipulator and tormentor. Though "Woolf displays a critical awareness that art . . . fails to capture the 'reality' of its subjects" (Gay 21), it is Lily's "business" as an artist "to combine and arrange" disparate elements into unity and harmony, according to Bell (8). But she must first do battle with her own demons. She faces the torment shared by every artist in the process of creation:

> It was in that moment's flight between the picture and her canvas that the demons set on her who often brought her to the verge of tears and made this passage from conception to work as dreadful as any down a dark passage for a child. Such she often felt herself—struggling against terrific odds to maintain her courage; to say, "But this is what I see; this is what I see." (19)

She also must confront her own special challenges as a female artist. Mr. Tansley offers his voice as a Schopenhauerian echo of female inferiority in the realm of genius, feeding Lily's own doubts with statements like, "Women can't paint, women can't write" (48), and "Women made civilisation impossible with all their 'charm,' all their silliness" (85). Little wonder when Lily confronts her awesome task of creation and unification she begins to paint "in that chill and windy way," noting that "the sun seems to give less heat" as she looks at her canvas (19).

Though an artist, Lily cannot stand apart from her object—the nihilistic nature in front of her and surrounding her: she must immerse herself in it before she can objectify it. This, Schopenhauer argues, is the source of artistic suffering. First in despair, then, as Lily looks upon her task she cries, "How aimless it was, how chaotic, how unreal it was" (146); "such were . . . the parts, but how to bring them together?" (147). Her response before this battle is to retreat, escape, not to surrender but to gather her arms: "She must escape somewhere, be alone somewhere" (147). Like Mrs. Ramsey, she too has decided to fight the world but with more powerful weapons than Mrs. Ramsey possessed: Lily sees her canvas as "a barrier" (149) between her and the world, literally using it to protect her from the imposing eyes of a Mr. Carmichael or a Mr. Tansley, and symbolically setting it up as a protective shield from the chaos while she strives to contain it. Her other weapon, the brush, she calls "the one dependable thing in a world of strife, ruin, and chaos" (150). Her battle cry, undoubtedly shared by all artists, is "In the midst of chaos there was shape," the belief that within "this eternal passing and flowing" there could be "stability" (161). This stability she knows as "the essential thing" (49), "the thing itself before it has been made anything" (193). She is seeking pure objectification of the will.

After committing herself to this task and surmounting the initial obstacles of self-doubt and fear, Lily realizes that her struggle has only begun. As with any immersion in life, once one has embarked upon the journey, the struggle lies ahead. Lily is fully aware of the connection between the creative process and living itself:

> One line placed on the canvas committed her to innumerable risks, to frequent and irrevocable decisions. All that in idea seemed simple became in practice immediately complex; as the waves shape themselves symmetrically from the cliff top, but to the swimmer among them are divided by steep gulfs, and foaming

crests. Still the risk must be run; the mark made. (157)

Lily's metaphoric representation of an artist as a swimmer in a chaotic sea reminds one of Schopenhauer's allusion to Virgil's *Aeneid* in his discussion of the special qualities of artists: "Singly they appear, swimming by in the vast waste of waves" (*Aeneid*, Book One, line 118; cited by Schopenhauer, *WWR* I, 236). But once the line has been painted, the artistic process has begun, and the artist is rewarded temporarily by a suspension of willing. As Marsh observes, the artist, "to understand life, or achieve a 'vision', . . . a sympathetic 'vibration' of rhythmical repetition must occur in the individual, in harmony with the rhythm that makes the 'shape' in life's chaos. To do this, self-consciousness must be abandoned. Lily loses consciousness of both the world around her and herself, and slips into 'the waters of annihilation'" (160). According to Schopenhauer, the artist, in the process of creation, escapes the fate of willfulness "if only for some few privileged moments. . . . Artists are lifted above the incessant becoming of will, its ever renewed lack and restlessness" (Desmond 114). Lily recognizes this state immediately:

> Here she was again, she thought, . . . drawn out of the gossip, out of the living, out of the community with people into the presence of this formidable ancient enemy of hers—this other thing, this truth, this reality, which suddenly laid hands on her, emerged stark at the back of appearances, and commanded her attention. (158)

Though Dowling sees the completion of Lily's painting at the end of the novel as "a true Hegelian synthesis" (150), the effect is not quite that positive. Nor is the modernist interpretation of Lily's painting as "her struggle to redeem the loss of Mrs. Ramsey on the aesthetic level" completely satisfactory (Minow-Pinkney 241). Even as Lily succeeds in bringing together the broken spirit of Mr. Ramsey with the fragmented, shining reflections of Mrs. Ramsey's spirit, the waves with the sea, the children with their father, she is uncertain of the lasting effect. Though she finds comfort in the ability of art to survive and endure ("'you' and 'I' and 'she' pass and vanish; nothing stays; all changes; but not words, not paint" [179]), she is also haunted by thoughts of her painting being hidden away or discarded to decay, like everything else in her experience, being "subject to the destructive effects of each new passing moment" (Dowling 151). Still, Dowling is correct in seeing an affirmation of the human spirit in the moment captured on canvas as Lily announces, "Yes, . . . I have had my vision" (209). Again Lily seems to echo Schopenhauer's representation of the victory of art over nature: the artist presents in the work of art "the beauty of the form which nature failed to achieve in a thousand attempts, and he places it before her, exclaiming as it were, 'This is what you desired to say!' And from the man who knows comes the echoing reply, 'Yes, that is it!'" (*WWR* I, 222).

Though Woolf may have rejected Schopenhauer outright and "refrain[ed] for ever" from his pages, her aesthetic novel belies her close affinity with both his aesthetic and world vision. Woolf and Schopenhauer shared a tragically acute understanding of human entrapment in the clutches of the world's will, and both saw art as the only salvation. Through the aesthetic theory of Bloomsbury, Fry in particular, and its roots in the pessimism of George Moore, Woolf held true to the Schopenhauerian objective of the novel, described by Fry himself in *The Artist and Psychoanalysis*:

> [Novels] note the inexorable sequence in life of cause and effect, they mark the total indifference of fate to all human desires, and they endeavor to derive precisely from that inexorability of fate an altogether different kind of pleasure—the pleasure which consists in the recognition of inevitable sequence; a pleasure which you see corresponds to the pleasure which we found in making the inevitable sequence of the notes of a tune. (12)

The pleasure we derive from art, then, is itself based on what we know to be our fate: endless repetition and sequence largely beyond our control. When the artist temporarily asserts control over the movement, there is pleasure. But

Schopenhauer and Woolf recognized that the pleasure has its roots in pain and suffering, just as life will always return to its source, the eternally repetitive, eternally moving will.

Chapter Four, Part One
Doris Lessing's *Children of Violence*:
The Schopenhauerian Education of Martha Quest

I

Doris Lessing inherited her interest in determinism, fatalism, and Schopenhauer from Olive Schreiner, one of her greatest literary influences. Furthermore, since Lessing asserts that *Martha Quest* is semi-autobiographical, she most likely first read Schopenhauer as an young woman in South Africa (*Under My Skin*, 162).[1] Lessing uses Schopenhauer as a philosophical touchstone for the character of Martha Quest, and several Schopenhauerian themes are at work throughout Lessing's fiction: the denial of our inextricable ties to the larger will, our moral obligation to the world community, and a desire to escape the prison of the individual will by projecting it outside of ourselves. The first two themes have been consistent threads through much of Lessing's work since her first novel, *The Grass is Singing* (1950), and were, no doubt, major reasons for her initial interest in Schopenhauer. Schopenhauer's view of morality as an awareness of a commitment to our fellow man and the subjugation of the personal will complements Lessing's leftist political beliefs as well as her spiritual interest in sufism.[2] Her objectives, however, are quite different from Schopenhauer's.

Lessing's novels certainly possess dark and pessimistic themes, but her desire for a better world, a phoenix in the ashes, is evident. Schopenhauer believed that no phoenix would materialize from the ashes of the world and that the best we can do is ease one another's suffering. Still, Schopenhauer and Lessing share the belief that a disregard for the collective good and attempts to disassociate oneself from it—outside of pure asceticism—lead to disaster. Lessing warns:

> [There are] two easy escapes of our time into false innocence. They are opposite sides of the same coin. One sees man as the isolated individual unable to communicate, helpless and solitary; the other as collective man with a collective conscience. Somewhere between these two, I believe, is a resting point, a place of decision, hard to reach and precariously balanced. . . . The point of rest should be the writer's recognition of man, the responsible individual, voluntarily submitting his will to the collective, but never finally. (*Small Personal Voice* 11-12)

Lessing's qualification ("never finally") separates her from Schopenhauer to the extent that he recognized no degree to which one must subordinate the will. But for Lessing's political beliefs, this qualification is essential.

Though she contends that the individual is sacred and deserves respect, Lessing believes that he/she will be best served by integrating personal needs with those of the collective whole. In her first novel, *The Grass is Singing*, the focus is on external racial tension between blacks and whites but also on the need to see ourselves in all people, places, and things—to see that we share the same essence. Lessing views racial prejudice as only one of many atrophies which hinder our ability to recognize a oneness among all things, a sense of shared pain, toil, suffering, and unrealized potential. When Mary Turner loses her mind and ultimately her life in *The Grass is Singing*, she has reached a point at which she simply cannot reconcile her own sexual and intellectual needs with the demands and limitations of her environment. This tension is a major focus of Lessing's entire body of work, and it is a curious, angry echo of Schopenhauer's views on female biological entrapment. As Roberta Rubenstein explains,

> In *The Grass is Singing* fragmentation is the response of Mary

>Turner's personality to the polarizations of reality along sexual and racial lines—antitheses that do not exist in the phenomenal world and that are only catalysts for her own inner divisions. The resulting breakdown emphasizes the disjunction between self and world through the fact that oppression has both political and psychological modalities, both of which are divisive. (*"Briefing"* 152)

Having been an independent, successful businesswoman before succumbing to the innate sexual urge to marry and reproduce (as well as the social pressures to "settle down"), Mary finds her human needs woefully ignored by a husband who cannot satisfy her physically, emotionally, or intellectually and by an environment which cannot sustain the expression of female autonomy. The only time Mary finds any outlet for her ambition and drive is when her husband falls ill and she must manage the farm. During this period of time she is able to channel her stifled sexual and intellectual impulses into constructive labor and is, temporarily, satisfied. She has in effect "voluntarily submitted" her individual will to a larger will and has found one of the few sources of peace offered by Schopenhauer and Lessing: the peace of losing oneself temporarily in the larger matter. When this outlet is no longer available, her longings return, now intensified and out of control, and her relentless will eventually leads to her destruction. This inability to express and satisfy the will must always, Schopenhauer stated, lead to suffering and torment: such is the nature of existence. And yet the struggle must continue, the struggle to endure and perhaps temporarily overcome the will by objectifying it.

This endless struggle, seen by Lessing as a primary activity in the modern woman's life, becomes a strong and fascinating theme in her fiction. After the publication of the first novel of the *Children of Violence* series, *Martha Quest*, Lessing expressed dismay at the confused and bizarre critical reaction to her work. Though she admitted to leftist, feminist, and sufist themes in the novel, she feared that her readers were missing her more direct purpose: "Not one critic has understood what I should have thought would be obvious from the first chapter, where I was at pains to state the theme very clearly: that this is a study of the individual conscience in its relation to the collective" (*Small Personal Voice* 14). It is this test of Schopenauerian morality and will—this tension between the individual and the *world as will*—which concerns Martha Quest as she move throughout the *Children of Violence* Bildungsroman but especially in the first two volumes when the character's will is at its most restless and defiant. Significantly, one of Martha's earliest literary mentors, one she initially ignores but comes to know very well through experience, is Schopenhauer. Martha Quest is a typically restless teenager in almost every way except that she grows up in British South Africa and reads such heavyweights as Nietzsche and Schopenhauer. At first she is rather indifferent to their philosophies, sensing that she knows already what these great men have to tell her, while at the same time suspecting that their words may exclude her: "She read like a bird collecting twigs for a nest. . . . And as she read she asked herself, What has this got to do with me? Mostly, she rejected; what she accepted she took instinctively" (200). Schopenhauer appeals quite readily to Martha's instinct, since even at her young age she finds that being a woman means a special kind of imprisonment of the will, an inescapable longing to experience what seems just out of reach, a never-ending yearning for satisfaction. She also understands what it means to feel excluded from the great ideas of her own culture, since these ideas were written largely by men, about men, and for men. Schopenhauer is certainly no exception.

The source of Martha's continually changing library is the pair of Cohen brothers who direct and advise her reading habits, satisfying her request for "books about the emancipation of women" with begrudging humor (56). She soon realizes that any interest in a "philosophy of her own" and the history of her own sex is an embarrassment, "naive, a hopeless self-exposure" (56). In essence, Martha learns that she must curb her desire to learn about her femaleness (after all, what could there be to learn?) and acquire a taste for the literary food served by men: Nietzsche, Schopenhauer, and the Cohen boys.

She does manage to digest some of this material and realizes, much to her discomfort, that she too has a will, a hunger, a need to understand her relationship to the outside world and to distinguish subjective experience from outer reality. As Rubenstein observes, 'What she reads also generates in her susceptible imagination ideals and philosophies that must inevitably be tested through her own experiences and often shattered" (*Novelistic Vision* 36). For instance, when Martha experiences sex for the first time, she is able to make the distinction between this particular, rather disappointing event and the "thing-in-itself": "For if the act fell short of her demand, that ideal, the thing-in-itself, that mirage, remained untouched, quivering exquisitely in front of her. . . . For this reason, then, it was easy for her to say that she was not disappointed, that everything still awaited her" (*Martha Quest* 184). Although Schopenhauer would refute the inherent optimism here and contend that Martha's "mirage" of the ideal is reality, that constant objective will, he would see that Martha has made a large step towards understanding that subjective reality is a fleeting shadow play of emotion and struggle within the eternal motion of the larger life force. Her sexual will has asserted itself, and she knows that it is only a fragment of the whole life process of longing, desire, growth, and struggle. She is neither surprised nor saddened by the fact that her will has not been satisfied, and she awaits further longing and continued expectation. She has never experienced complete satisfaction at any point so far in her young life, and she senses, though in a naive, romantic way, that she will never fully become one with the "thing-in-itself."

What this "thing" is and where it is located is a source of some consideration for Martha, as it is for most young people as they begin to question their individual relationship to outer reality. Is "it" within or without? One clue to her own power and ability to "objectify" reality as her own creation is the sense of an inner source of her youthful pessimism. When she feels especially depressed or confused, she discovers an ability "to focus a dispassionate eye on that misery. This detached observer, felt perhaps as a clear-lit space situated just behind the forehead, was the gift of the Cohen boys at the station, who had been lending her books for the last two years" (8). Here Martha attributes her ability to see her emotions as separate from her essential self to her reading of the determinists. At this point Martha is at the stage of seeing her inner, individual will as largely negative, as something that causes her misery and yet, somehow, reveals clarity, existing in that "clear-lit space." She is struggling with the Freudian notion of the conscious and unconscious and the respective positive and negative connotations associated with them. Though, as we have seen, Freud recognized a debt to Schopenhauer's will in the concept of his unconscious, both Schopenhauer and Lessing would need to point out the difficulties in the Freudian landscape.

> The Freudians describe the conscious as a small lit area, all white, and the unconscious as a great dark marsh full of monsters. In their view, the monsters reach up, grab you by the ankles, and try to drag you down. But the unconscious can be what you make of it, good or bad, helpful or unhelpful. (*Small Personal Voice* 67)

Lessing's unconscious (i.e., Schopenhauer's will) is indeed a thing of clarity as well as misery for Martha and continues to assert itself in both of these functions throughout her evolution.[3] She will find very little rest between the two extremes.

Like many of her literary predecessors, Martha discovers as escape from the will in her own "spot of time," a Romantic "moment" in nature. Martha is simply walking in a quiet area when she feels a change taking place:

> there was a slow integration, during which she, and the little animals, and the moving grasses, and the sun-warmed trees, and the slopes of shivering silvery mealies, and the great dome of the blue light overhead, and the stones of the earth under her feet, became one, shuddering together in a dissolution of dancing atoms. (52)

During this rather pantheistic experience, much like those of Virginia Woolf and

Wordsworth (Sukenick 107), Martha is at once overcome with the rush of life which dissolves all into one and with a sense of her own insignificance: "For that space of time (which was timeless) she understood quite finally her own smallness, the unimportance of humanity" (*Martha Quest* 52-53). It is a moment in which Martha "experiments with the possibilities of surrendering identities, of obscuring the distinction between the self and the not-self" (Rigney 139). This experiment echoes the very essence of Schopenhauer's philosophy of man and nature: man, while being the entire will in microcosm, is also nothing as an individual:

> Nature has her centre in every individual, for each one is the entire will-to-live. Therefore, even if this individual is only an insect or a worm, nature herself speaks out of it as follows: 'I alone am all in all; in my maintenance is everything involved; the rest may perish, it is really nothing.' Thus nature speaks from the **particular** standpoint, from that of self-consciousness, and to this is due the **egoism** of every living thing. On the other hand, from the universal standpoint, from that of the consciousness of other things, and thus from that of objective knowledge . . . nature speaks thus: 'the individual is nothing and less than nothing. I destroy millions of individuals every day for sport and pastime; I abandon their fate to chance. . . . every day I produce millions of new individuals without any diminution of my productive power. . . . The individual is nothing.' (*WWR* II, 599-600)

This surrender of individual identity to the larger will is one of only a few possible sources of peace in Schopenhauer's view, and usually, as in Martha's case, the relief is only temporary. The individual will asserts itself once again as Martha finds herself in a loveless marriage burdened by an unwanted pregnancy.

II

This pregnancy and its effects on Martha are the focus of *A Proper Marriage*, part two of *Children of Violence*. The emphasis in the novel on the necessary demands of the will to perpetuate itself through human reproduction illustrates how deeply Martha's childhood reading of Schopenhauer influenced her later perceptions of her body, her mind, and her role in society.

From the outset of her marriage Martha finds herself in a struggle to maintain some sort of individuality, and from the beginning she knows the battle was lost. Weeks after becoming Douglas Knowell's wife, she observes with some astonishment that "she had not been alone for five minutes since her marriage" (4). A constant sense of loss engulfs her; she realizes at once that her marriage is a mistake, but she is also aware of the question which is implied by this "failure" as a wife: if a woman is not fit for marriage, what, indeed, is she fit for? The tension between her marital unhappiness and her confusion about this tension gives Martha "the feeling of someone caught in a whirlpool" (17). At one point she observes "there were moments when she felt she was strenuously held together by nothing more than an act of will" (63).

Since there appears to be no escape from this whirlpool, Martha attempts to submit, a decision heartily endorsed by her Schopenhauerian education. She remembers, for example, that good comes from concentration on the not-self, "a willingness to devote oneself utterly to another's life" (22). Like a modern day Dorothea Brooke, Martha submits, first to her husband's needs, trying to be the ideal wife, lover, and status symbol, then to her social circle, volunteering for charity functions and other activities appropriate for the average woman trying to fill the hours between the departure and arrival of a husband: "Some instinct to conform had dictated that she must quell her loathing, as at entering a trap. . . . She was instinctively compliant, enthusiastic, and took every step into bondage with affectionate applause from Douglas" (250). As the threat of the World War encroaches, Martha listens with envy to the conversations of the men, her husband included, who are planning to enlist: "they were all longing to be swallowed up in something larger than themselves" (67). Submission, however, is not an easy task for Martha, and it eventually leads to rebellion. She decides finally that "the mere idea of submitting herself to the intentions of anybody else must be repulsed" (23). She wants to escape "this appalling feeling of flatness, staleness, and futility" which had become her life (34). She wanted involvement, a life of "conversation and ideals" (33), of true commitment to something important, a cause. She decides to leave Douglas in search of this cause. That, at last, will give vent to this raging will inside of her, "this undefined craving and hollowness, a sort of hunger" (64).

Then, she finds she is pregnant. Life instantly becomes the trap she always feared it was. She realizes that her pregnancy is not a result of carelessness, that she and Douglas had failed to use the precautionary measures made available to them, that they had probably subconsciously wanted this child. Subconsciously. The word sounds like betrayal to Martha—self-betrayal. If she cannot trust herself, her own impulses, what was the point of any struggle? "For what was the use of thinking, of planning," she asks herself, "if emotions one did not recognize at all worked their own way against you" (103)? If one's own instincts have a will and an agenda of their own, are we all not merely victims of biology and the will itself, "mere pawns in the hands of an old fatality" (94)? Martha had read the terrifying answer to this question years earlier, and Schopenhauer had offered her little comfort:

> The growing attachment of two lovers is in itself in reality the will-to-live of the new individual, an individual they can and want to produce. . . . They feel the longing for an actual union and fusion into a single being, in order then to go on living only as this being. (*WWR* II, 536)

So she and Douglas had been trapped from the beginning.

Feeling cheated out of a destiny of her own making, Martha believes that her pregnancy forces her into place in the march of time and that her life will be indistinguishable from all those before and after her in the pathetic parade:

> She could not meet a young man or woman without looking anxiously for the father and mother: that was how they would end, there was no escape for them. She could not meet an elderly person without wondering what the unalterable influences had been that had created them just so. She could take no step, perform no action, no matter how apparently new and unforeseen, without the secret fear that this new and arbitrary thing would turn out to be part of the inevitable process she was doomed to. (77)

True to the Schopenhauerian concept of human nature, Martha responds to her "doom" first by denying her entrapment, trying to convince herself "it was in her power to cut the cycle" (95). Then, a sense of hopelessness follows: "she was gripped by a lethargy so profound that in fact she spent most of her time on the divan, thinking of nothing" (98). The intensity of the whirlpool overwhelmed her: "she felt caught up in an immense impersonal tide which paid no attention to her" (101).

Martha's unintentional acceptance of her fate is as horrifying as her biological victimization. Seemingly against her will, she realizes "that in some part of herself she was already weakening towards this baby" (102). This, too, seems a betrayal. The "maternal instincts" she had heard about, the proper functions of the female animal which Schopenhauer had described, were being played out in her body, in her mind, and she was losing the ability to fight them. "The imprisoned thing moving in her flesh" had claimed her, and now she was giving herself up willingly to it (102). The kinship she establishes with it becomes not one of mother and child but of fellow prisoners writhing against the walls of will which enfold both of them. As "the creature" becomes a human being inside of her, Martha feels it "seething and striving like a wrestler" (137-38). Schopenhauer makes the same connection between the unborn child, its willful activities, and its sense of imprisonment: The new-born child moves violently, screams and cries; it wills most vehemently, although it does not yet know what it wills. . . . It rages like a prisoner against the walls and bars of his dungeon (*WWR* II, 234-35). The kicks and pulls Martha begins to feel from within seem to her only to manifest the totality of mankind's struggle against its fate: "inside her stomach the human race had fought and raised its way through another million years of history" (113).

The pregnancy places Martha in another struggle between her desire to maintain some individuality and the seemingly overwhelming urge to surrender to the whirlpool of the will: "One part of herself was sunk in the development of the creature, appallingly slow, frighteningly inevitable, a process which she could not alter or hasten, and which dragged her back into the impersonal blind urges of creation" (127). Here Martha echoes Schopenhauer's insistence on the role of the "blind will" in human reproduction, the sexual act being the purest expression of the will-to-live. On the other side of the struggle, in direct opposition to this blind force, Martha feels determined to "keep brightly burning that lamp above the dark blind sea which was motherhood. She would *not* allow herself to be submerged" (127). What Martha fails to realize at this point is that her desire to fulfill her function as a mother and her longing to survive as an individual both stem from the same source and share the same objective: the continuance of the species, the only objective of the will, according to Schopenhauer. Hence, Martha "felt a determination to continue, a curiosity perhaps, an intention to endure, but no delight" (129). She is merely fulfilling her role to survive in order to reproduce, Schopenhauer would argue: survival itself is essential, not her "delight" in surviving.

The chapter on Martha's labor and the child Caroline's birth can be read as an extended metaphor for the individual's relationship with the will. Martha is presented initially as the strong, willful individual of the first two novels of *Children of Violence*. She is determined to handle the situation with grace and dignity: she refuses to anticipate submission to pain. As the chapter concludes, Lessing shows us a woman broken by inescapable pain, a force so strong that it is immune to her struggles and determination. Like the will itself, the pain of giving birth to another will is beyond Martha's comprehension, so much so that during the brief respites from the pain, she is enraged at her inability to remember it, even to imagine what it had been like only moments before. Lessing's point here, it seems, is the futility of a battle with an enemy whose strength cannot be seen, measured, or imagined. And yet the battle must take place. Martha is "astonished and indignant at the violence" of her enemy; "the pain had swallowed *her* up." The child herself seems at once in league with the enemy and with its victim, Martha: "tight, stiff, cautious, she felt the baby knot and propel itself down; it recoiled and slackened, and she with it. . . . it was as if she and the baby were being wrung out together by a pair of enormous steel hands" (143). At least now Martha had an image for the power to which she had been forced to submit: the enormous steel hands of pure will.

The remainder of *A Proper Marriage* is devoted to what Lessing appropriately calls the "contests of will" which follow Caroline's birth (202). Martha becomes increasingly depressed at the thought of Caroline perpetuating "the direct line of matriarchy she so feared" (151), and she fears that unless Caroline is somehow freed from a traditional upbringing, "she would certainly grow up to be like these women about her, a dull housewife with no purpose in life but to continue the cycle of procreation" (152). Martha is also horrified at her occasional impulses, fed by pressures from Douglas, to have another child: "Martha knew her female self was sharply demanding that she should start the cycle of birth again" (251). Concurrent with these realizations is Martha's discovery of a leftist political movement forming in her small African community. She becomes more and more excited by the movement and falls in love with one of its leaders. Convinced that she will never be a "proper" mother to Caroline and equally certain that the child will flourish without the "poisoning influence" of the stifling maternal demands under which Martha always struggled, she walks out of her marriage to embrace the cause she believes is her destiny (204).

Though Martha's rejection of her role as wife and mother may reveal an admirable, radical self-awareness, Schopenhauer would argue that she has merely traded one form of imprisonment for another. Her desire to lose herself in a cause is a logical and not entirely useless impulse, according to Schopenhauer, since any denial of the individual will for the larger good results in some diminishment of suffering. But Martha's motivations are those of eternal change and revolution, a desire to end the cycle which has victimized her, a feminist drive to change the world for women through rebellion and political restructuring. This is not, as Martha believes, a longing "to hurl [herself] 'for once and for all' into complete self-abnegation" (313), but rather a longing to assert her will in less domestic directions. It will lead to intense suffering and disappointment, as all human activity must, according to Schopenhauer, which does not recognize the futility of any struggle against the indestructible will.

III

The third novel in Lessing's *Children of Violence* series, *A Ripple from the Storm*, recounts Martha Quest's involvement with the Communist movement in Africa during World War II. Following her divorce, Martha embraces a small group of varied personalities joined under the banner of Communism and dedicated to the creation of a utopia of sexual and racial equality, a government of the workers, and a global economic and political unity. Martha totally surrenders herself to this cause, ignoring personal needs and abandoning friends and relatives who do not fit into her new mode of living. Her affairs with men associated with the movement leave her as confused and unsatisfied as her married life did, but she dismisses her own disappointments as unimportant in the larger scheme of world crisis. In short, she attempts to destroy her individual will through absorption into the "other," the larger life force. What she accomplishes, however, is complete entanglement in a trap of optimism and historicism.

Schopenhauer would applaud the idea of the one in many, the one representing the whole, since this is the very essence of his argument of the will. He would also concur with the objective of the destruction of ego, self, for the betterment of the whole, "an all-comprehensive compassion for the whole of humanity" (Ripple 38). But to imagine that this sense of oneness, this understanding of the unity of all things has the power to liberate people from suffering is a trap, often identified by Schopenhauer as optimism:

> At bottom, optimism is the unwarranted self-praise of the real author of the world, namely, the will-to-live, which complacently mirrors itself in its work. Accordingly, optimism is not only a false but also a pernicious doctrine, for it presents life as a desirable state and man's happiness as its aim and object. Starting from this, everyone then believes he has the most legitimate claim to happiness and enjoyment. If, as usually happens, these do not fall to his lot, he believes that he suffers an injustice, in fact he misses the whole point of his existence: whereas it is far more correct to regard work, privation, misery, and suffering, crowned by death, as the aim and object of our life . . . , since it is these that lead to the denial of the will-to-live. (*WWR* II, 584)

If we search ourselves, our optimism will always ring false, Schopenhauer contends, and will reveal itself as flour paste covering an ugly deformity:

> Optimism . . . conflicts with the obvious misery of existence. . . . The oft-repeated doctrine of a progressive development of mankind to an ever higher perfection, or generally of any kind of becoming by means of the world-process, is opposed to the a priori view that, up to any given point of time, an infinite time has already elapsed, and consequently all that is supposed to come with time is bound to have existed already. (*WWR* II, 184)

Resisting the haunting idea that she is merely a pawn in the endless march of time, Martha fights with all her power to ignore the false ringing of her hopefulness, but it remains a constant tone throughout the novel.

One voice which contributes to this refrain belongs to Mr. Maynard, a middle-aged acquaintance of Martha's who has known her since before her marriage. Completely disdainful of the Communist movement arising in his village, he represents the voice of Schopenhauerian fatalism and serves as a disturbing reminder for Martha of her early understanding of the futility of existence. It is partly Maynard's sporadic conversations and meetings with Martha which feed the fire of her disillusionment and doubts about Communism, relationships, and life in general. "What," Maynard asks Martha, "is history? A record of misery, brutality, and stupidity. That's all. That's all it will ever be" (46), echoing Schopenhauer's observation, 'What history relates is in fact only the long, heavy, confused dream of mankind" (*WWR* II, 443). Maynard shares Schopenhauer's disdain for historicism as a guide for improving the lot of mankind. His question to Martha is placed in direct opposition to a speech at Martha's Communist group in which she is told, "We have the supreme good fortune and the responsibility to be living at a time when mankind takes the first great step forward from barbarity and chaos of unplanned production to the sunlight of socialism" (53). This, Schopenhauer would insist, is the dogma of the idealist: since history and time itself are mere representations created in the mind of the individual, they are indeed illusions which will cease to exist with the individual. Belief in history is a belief in "soap bubbles":

> Fools imagine that something is supposed to come into existence. . . . They take the world to be perfectly real, and set its purpose in miserable earthly happiness. . . . Such happiness is yet a hollow, deceptive, frail, and wretched thing, out of which neither constitutions, legal systems, steam engines, nor telegraphs can ever make anything that is essentially better. . . . The true philosophy of history thus consists in the insight that, in spite of all these endless changes and their chaos and confusion, we yet always have before

> us only the same, identical, unchangeable essence. (*WWR* II, 443-44)

History in the Hegelian sense for Schopenhauer does not exist, and historical optimism is a dangerous fancy, leading to a strengthened will-to-live and, hence, increased suffering.

The battle lines drawn, then, between a fatalism of her past which appeals to Martha's deepest understanding and a new and inviting optimism, Martha surrenders to her longing for an escape from the world view of Maynard (and earlier mentors) into a state of simple, if self-deceptive, trust in human autonomy over the ageless, senseless march of history:

> It seemed to her this unhurrying voice was cutting the past from her, that ugly past which Mr. Maynard had described. . . . It was all finished. She was feeling a comprehensive compassion: for the pitiful past, and for the innumerable unhappy people of the world whom she was pledging herself to deliver. . . . She was returned to a knowledge of the thrust and push of knitting natural forces which had grappled with the substance of her own flesh, to become part of it. . . . So she had felt years ago when the Cohen boys at the station put books into her hands. (53-54)

And what of the other lessons contained in these books? What of the darker, fatalistic warnings of the determinists, Nietzsche, Schopenhauer? "She might still admire the great men she had been used to admire," Martha told herself, but "they had been misguided" (54).

Martha is soon reminded that all human endeavor is destined to corruption and failure and, as Schopenhauer states, history is only the sum total of individual human weakness. She sees her small group of dedicated radicals disband because of petty differences of personality and major disagreements of party policy. She gradually senses the futility of their small struggles within the larger machine of war, racial prejudice, and enduring human nature. Even when her conscious mind tries to fight her growing fears of the hopelessness of mankind, her subconscious reminds her of the indestructible essence of human action, driven by the endless will, creating more and more horror. She dreams of venturing deep into the earth. As she descends, she is startled by a projection on the side of the rock,

> an immense lizard, an extinct saurian that had been imprisoned a thousand ages ago in the rock. It was petrified. . . . Martha looked again and saw that its eye was steadily regarding her with a sullen and patient query. It was a scaly ancient eye, filmed over with mine dust, a sorrowful eye. It's alive, she thought. It's alive after so many centuries. And it will take centuries more to die. (85)

The world's misery can be ignored and buried for a time, the will can be seduced into a false sleep temporarily, but Schopenhauer would remind Martha that both live in the recesses of our existence, and they are indestructible.

As her dream concludes, Martha hopes to free the lizard from its entrapment. Similarly, as her dream of deliverance through communal life dies, she attempts to find peace through the identity of a powerful leader of the movement. She marries the German dissident Anton to save him from gossip and scrutiny resulting from their affair, and she attempts to become what he demands: a loyal subject of Joseph Stalin, and of Anton himself. Soon Martha feels "caged and hemmed in" (111) as she had with Douglas; "she was again full of violent dissatisfaction" (114). As the ebb and flow of her will works its motion, Martha feels the need for action just as she decides to "settle down," and dreams once again force her to face the knowledge she has rejected:

> Already she was feeling, under the pressure of the snapping jaws of impatience, the need to move forward. . . . She went to sleep depressed and dreamed she was with Maisie [a female comrade], who was due to have her baby, and they were hurrying from door to door trying to find a house which would take her in. But the doors remained closed against them both. (175)

With no escape in sight, then, Martha resigns herself to an emotionally and sexually unsatisfying marriage with Anton. As the novel closes, Martha has failed on several levels: she has been unable to find a favorable replacement for the life she rejected when she left her marriage; she has entered into another marriage doomed to failure ("The cast had changed, the play was the same" [*Landlocked* 108]); she has lost faith in the one cause she believed in; and she is no closer to her goals of establishing some sense of identity and autonomy. In fact, she has drawn no concrete picture of herself at all. "Why is it," she asks herself, " I listen for the echoes of other people in my voice and what I do all the time? The fact is, I'm not a person at all, I'm nothing yet—perhaps I never will be" (260). Having come full circle back to the fatalism of her youth, Martha expresses a Schopenhauerian conclusion at the end of *A Ripple from the Storm*: "It was inevitable that everything should have happened in exactly the way it had happened: no one could have behaved differently [and] everything that had happened was unreal, grotesque, and irrelevant" (261). Still, one hope for the future, her own individual future, remains—in the form of yet another man, a "faceless man who waited in the wings of the future, waiting to free the Martha who was in cold storage." Martha "restored her own wholeness by resting in imagination on the man who would enter her life and make her what she knew she could be" (230). Liberation, her Schopenhauerian education should have told her, does not come so easily.

IV

Dreams continue to inform Martha of her fears and longings in *Landlocked*, the fourth novel in *Children of Violence*. They are dreams of abandonment, restless seas, and lost friends. When she opens her eyes, she is welcomed by the world of her nightmares: she is trapped in a marriage of convenience and left without a cause for which to fight. She continues to see her life as a waiting game, waiting for the man who would "unify her elements, a man who would be like a roof, or like a fire burning in the centre of the empty space" (30). She knows she has to survive: "this phase of her life was sticking it out, waiting, keeping herself ready for when 'life' would begin" (13). As the war ends, Martha sees the entire world in physical or emotional ruins, and she cannot cope with more than the idea of simply surviving—and waiting—from day to day:

> The continuity of Martha now was in a determination to survive—like everyone else in the world . . . a tension of the will that was like a small flickering of light, like the perpetual tiny dance of lightning on the horizon from a storm so far over the earth's curve it could only show reflected on the sky. (14)

When she finally discovers the man she has waited for, Thomas, a married leftist radical, she soon realizes that he too will leave her to search for his own peace, only to die alone in a foreign country.

Amidst the chaos of racial strife in South Africa, Martha struggles to regain some sense of wholeness as she sees an ineffectual Communist group once more try to save the day. And once again Martha sees her hopes of a new world "after the war" dashed and faces the probability that the human race is indeed doomed to repeat its tragic cycle over and over again. Nothing seems ordered or logical; chance appears to have been responsible for everything, even her own survival:

> Every fibre of Martha's body, everything she thought, every movement she made, everything she was, was because she had been born at the end of one world war, and had spent all her adolescence in the atmosphere of preparations for another which had lasted five years and inflicted such wounds on the human race that no one had any idea of what the results would be. [Though] Martha did not believe in violence Martha was the essence of violence, she had been conceived, bred, fed, and reared on violence. (195)

Mr. Maynard, perhaps, was right, she concludes, as she sums up her life as "very crude and ridiculous" (32).

Still, her affair with Thomas does unify her, not only with herself but with her relationship to humanity. She sees a Schopenhauerian connection between her own suffering and the lot of the whole human race. Though this causes her much pain, it also permits a sense of oneness with the world that had always before seemed a stranger to her:

> the soul of the human race, that part of the mind which has no name, is not called Thomas and Martha, which holds the human race as frogspawn is held in jelly—that part of Martha and of Thomas was twisted and warped, was part of a twist and a damage—she should no more disassociate herself from the violence done her, than a tadpole can live out of water. Forty-odd million human beings had been murdered, deliberately or from carelessness, from lack of imagination; these people had been killed yesterday, in the last dozen years, they were dying now, as she stood under the tree, and these deaths were marked on her soul.
> ... She felt her pulse beat like warnings of time passing. (196)

The passing of time is marked for Martha by a different kind of death as well. She witnesses the death of the idealism of her youth in the lives of her former comrades, now in their thirties, settled, complacent and, to Martha's mind, beaten: "Lives that appear to them meaningless, wasted, hang around their necks like decaying carcasses. They are hypnotized into futility by self-observation. . . . And it is these people who [were] at twenty the liveliest, the most intelligent, the most promising" (205). Martha fears she is one of them.

Landlocked ends with Thomas' truly Schopenhauerian testament, "The world is a lump of filth crawling with vermin" (271), written in his journal shortly before his death. With these words echoing in her mind, Martha embarks on her own final journey, back to England.

V

The fifth and final novel in the Martha Quest series, *The Four-Gated City* (1969), can be seen as a culmination of all of the darker themes in the previous four parts. Once in England, Martha begins a journey of desperation, a fight against all of the forces within and around her which threaten madness, fragmentation, and death. *The Four-Gated City* is perhaps the most pessimistic of all the Martha Quest novels, reinforcing as it does the Schopenhauerian premise of life as inescapable longing and confused purpose. But unlike the previous works, it focuses on the various ways people attempt to escape these longings rather than on the source of the longings, the will.

The complacency Martha observed in her once radical comrades continues to be a source of aggravation and fear in *The Four-Gated City*. Martha begins to realize that this surrender to the world is actually a means of escaping the torment of senseless struggle. Everywhere—in individuals as well as society as a whole—Martha senses a cold abstraction, a state she likens to sedation or hypnotism. She finds England "a country absorbed in myth, doped and dozing and dreaming" (16). She pleads with her lethargic friends to wake up to the dangers of self-destruction through denial: "You all seem to me to be—you're drugged, you're hypnotized, you don't seem to be able to see facts when they're in front of you" (29). And her initial goal for herself as the novel opens is to avoid their fate, "to live in such a way that I don't just—turn into a hypnotized animal" (94). Not until she enters the household of Mark and his mentally disturbed wife Linda does she realize the advantages of hypnosis as an escape from the will.

The often astute, sometimes irrational Linda becomes another of Martha's female mentors in her odyssey of self-discovery. Linda teaches Martha both the advantages and the horrors offered by madness and loss of will. Linda explains to Martha that insanity is in fact a useful form of escape from wifehood, motherhood, and all other demands placed on women by society. In a state of madness, Linda tells Martha, "you don't have any will, you don't want anything, you just want to sit about" (303). As Martha becomes more involved with Linda's life, she ventures dangerously close to accepting madness as her escape from a will which in the past led her to disastrous relationships, political and social rebellion, and an unsatisfactory self-image. The possibility of "not wanting anything," a period of self-denial, is extremely inviting to Martha, who is filled with longing. She equates this condition with a tune which runs through her head: "Mother must I go on dancing? Infuriating, ridiculous, banal. . . . Always. Mother, must I go on dancing. Yes. She knew only too well she had to go on dancing" (38). Madness, Linda promised, could stop the dance.

The strongest symptom of Martha's pending madness is her inability to remember the past. She seems to have forgotten long periods of time in her past as well as recent events gone by: "Whole areas of Martha's life had slipped away (206). This inability—or unwillingness—to recall one's past is the central point of madness, according to Schopenhauer. He viewed the state of madness as directly related to an interruption, either temporary or permanent, in the intellect's objective to satisfy the will. This is most often caused, as is likely in Martha's case, by the intellect's attempt to block certain painful memories or failures from itself, but also for the sake of the will to live:

> Real soundness of mind consists in perfect recollection. . . . If certain events or circumstances are wholly suppressed for the intellect, because the will cannot bear the sight of them; and then, if the resultant gaps are arbitrarily filled up for the sake of the necessary connection; we then have madness. For the intellect has given up its nature to please the will; the person then imagines what does not exist. But the resultant madness then becomes
> . . . the last resource of worried and tormented nature, i.e., of the will. (*WWR* II, 399-401)

One person stands in the way of Martha's—and Linda's—"last resource" of madness. Dr. Lamb, a psychologist, is unmistakenly associated with the will itself, a force which calls Martha back to herself, a power which is all-pervasive and inescapable. For these reasons, Martha is afraid of him, while also drawn to him:

> The central fact here was that no one approached Dr. Lamb unless he had to. In approaching Dr. Lamb, one approached power. It was hard to think of a power like it, in its inclusiveness, its arbitrariness, its freedom to behave as it wished, without checks from other places or powers. (306)

Schopenhauer would ascribe the same characteristics to the will: inclusive, arbitrary, without restraint. Because of his authority, Dr. Lamb represents a two-fold threat to the unstable Martha: his power can prevent her from the escape she seeks (he can possibly "cure" her emotional illness) or he can place her in a position in which she must surrender totally. In short, he could have her committed:

> Inside the dozens of mental hospitals scattered up and down the country, built like prisons, were many thousands of people who had been straight-jacketed, forcibly fed, kept in padded cells, beaten (in fact, the central fact, had had their wills broken), and were now derelict, "deteriorated." (308)

The imprisonment of madness, "social" madness which in some way must be contained, controlled, restrained, seems to Martha just another state of frustrated potential. Even in madness, she would be seeking another state—a state of private, internal freedom in which she would be at peace. But the often drugged, institutionalized Linda serves as a reminder of the horrible price paid for a highly unsatisfactory escape from life.

Turning away from Dr. Lamb as well as her brief journey into Linda's world of mental illness, Martha is more determined than ever to avoid the torture of existence as she sees it. A second Schopenhauerian option Martha explores is annihilation of self through sex. Lessing's examination of the sexual act in *The*

Four-Gated City is a vivid example of Schopenhauer's concept of the will's role in sex. Essentially for Schopenhauer, the will is perfectly expressed or realized in the sexual act. The nature of the will is identical to the nature of sex; both are blind, irrational, ends in themselves. Because Martha discovers in sex a complete surrender of self to the will, she is able to find a great deal of peace she seeks within the sexual act.

The two main sexual relationships in the novel are between Martha and Mark and Martha and the hedonistic artist, Jack. Through both men Martha learns that sex can be the most mystical of experiences while serving as a practical means of escape from self. Sex is described throughout the novel in strong Schopenhauerian language, relating it as Schopenhauer does to the pure expression of will. For Martha, sex takes on various roles, all of them related to a loss of self, a surrender of control in the midst of a greater power, and an integration into the one force moving all things, the will:

> Sex was . . . a power, a force, which, when held and controlled, took both [lovers] up and over and away from any ordinary consciousness into—an area where no words could be of use
> . . . . The first movement of body in body was not a willed one, from his side or hers, but came from, was impelled by, was on, the rhythm of blood-beat and breath . . . like an animal impulse toward another, a warmth. Sex, heart, the currents of automatic body were one now, together. (58-59)

It is now the irrational nature of sex which appeals to Martha, and she protests any attempt to intellectualize it:

> We don't understand the first thing about what goes on, not the first thing. "Make love," "make sex," "orgasms," "climaxes"—it was all nonsense, words, sounds, invented by half-animals who understood nothing at all. Great forces as impersonal as thunder or lightning or sunlight or the movement of oceans being

> contracted and heaped and rolled in their beds by the moon, swept through bodies, and now she knew quite well why Mark had come blindly upstairs to the nearest friendly body, being in the grip of this force. (471)

Martha becomes aware for the first time of sex as life-giver, the source of "feverish electricity," "high energy," all being (380); "she felt as if she had been connected to a dynamo, the centre of her life" (61). She is astounded by the hypnotized ones who continue to regard "sex as the drainer, the emptier, instead of the maker of energy" (61).

But like all other Schopenhauerian methods of pacifying, objectifying, or denying the will, sex too often becomes yet another conscious act of the will, another longing, another insatiable need. For Martha, it becomes the enemy. Her need for sex becomes synonymous with her need for another, her desire to be loved, and a dependence on others, instead of momentary absorption in the sex energy. This leads to imprisonment for Martha: "Now she was invaded by sex. One only had to think: A man, I need a man, and sex invades in its battalions" (192). And her vulnerability to love places her in the defensive position in this battle, this "silent, desperate act of—survival" (379). When love complicates the sexual act, Schopenhauer would agree, sex becomes conscious willing, no different from the will to eat, drink, sleep, etc. In other words, it loses its potential for release and escape and becomes another form of objectified will which we strive against: "If one is in love with a man," Martha realizes, "'in love' or in the condition of loving, then there comes to life that hungry, never-to-be-fed, never-at-peace woman who needs and wants and must have" (286). Martha fears this woman more than anything else.

As the novel closes, Martha has reached a state of acceptance which resembles the fatalism she fought so ardently in her younger years. She exits the novel with the same kinds of observations of human beings with which she began. Looking at the people and things around her, Martha concludes that given the nature of man, the evil of the world is inescapable: "Good Lord, she found herself thinking, for the thousandth time, what kind of a race is this that chooses, inevitably and invariably, or so it seemed, the ugly, the graceless?" (32). Even sex, her last bastion against the resurgence of the conscious will, is subject to human corruption: "The impersonal sea could become the thousand volts of hate as easily as it could become love—much more easily, human beings being what they are" (471). She bases these conclusions on her Schopenhauerian theory of doomed human activity:

> A baby is born with infinite possibilities for being good. But there's no escaping it, it's like having to go down to a pit, a terrible dark, blind pit, and then you fight your way up and out
>
> .... The mistake is, to think there is a way of not having to fight your way out. Everyone has to. (68)

Striving is indeed the one everlasting activity of life, Schopenhauer states, and it ends in futility. Martha's fatalism is based not only on her awareness of the endless struggle of life but on its uselessness: "It had not mattered what they had planned, since human beings were the prisoners of events" (125). Here Martha returns to the feeling of biological and social determinism she experienced during and after her pregnancy: even her own instincts lead her in predetermined directions. A will seemingly separate from her but also within her dictates her movements: "Looking back," Martha concludes, "we think we've made decisions—it's something else that makes them" (70)

That "something else," Schopenhauer's will, forces Martha into this state of acceptance which brings her, perhaps, a kind a peace. She is not hypnotized; she knows now that "life is all war" (150). But she has learned that there is such a thing as understanding one's inescapable role in the fray. Through this understanding one may claim the only possible victory: an ability to comfort one's self and others in the midst of the common struggle of mankind.

Chapter Four, Part Two
Doris Lessing's *The Fifth Child*: The Will Personified

Doris Lessing has always been interested in how children reflect both the nakedness of our souls as well as the vulnerability of society as a whole. The *Children of Violence* series traces the growth of a young girl as she learns to adapt to the almost overwhelming ugliness of modern existence on personal, social, and political levels. True to her sufist beliefs, however, Lessing ends *Children of Violence* with the implication that the children of the future will be "higher up on the evolutionary scale with extrasensory organs" (Pickering 191), children who will develop whatever faculties are necessary to adapt to the challenges of the modern world. However, in Lessing's 1988 novel, *The Fifth Child*, her message seems very different and much more pessimistic, "hypothesizing here a reversion to primitive states of being . . . the underside of the cosmic view she has struggled so painfully toward" (191). Lessing seems now to have set loose the forces of the will which she had tried to rationalize and contain in previous novels. In fact, the "cosmic view" presented in *The Fifth Child* is Schopenhauer's view, and the fifth child, Ben, instead of being the promise of Hegelian progress, is more akin to Yeats's beast which stalks the holy city, that ambiguous harbinger of the future who holds no promise except to always exist. The fifth child is the pure personification of the will.

In *The Fifth Child* the personification of the will takes the form of a son, a literal creation of two idealistic, traditionalist parents, Harriet and David Lovatt.

David and Harriet married with the objective of creating a "fortress" of tradition, old-fashioned values, and Victorian stability (20). This fortress would be filled with children, as many as six, maybe more, in direct contradiction to the cautious reproductive trend of the modern world. They would shield themselves and their children from the ugliness of the world known as "progress," including the violence, the sterility, the wasteland of emotions "out there." Both Harriet and David planned their lives and ruled their passions to this end. Before their marriage their relationship is virtually passionless. They sleep together, but barely touch, with no overwhelming desire for intercourse: children conceived out of wedlock are not part of the plan. But once married, their lust—to reproduce rather than to make love—cannot be contained. Their first four children are conceived and born in rapid succession, leaving Harriet tired but satisfied in her purpose. According to plan, their large Victorian home is soon filled with the sounds of child rearing and the holiday visits of extended family members who repeatedly voice their concerns over the Lovatt's lifestyle. Harriet and David listen patronizingly to their relatives' warnings about the cost of raising children and the dangers to their own health.

With Harriet's fifth pregnancy, however, comes an invasion of the fortress from within, "a challenge . . . to destiny" (27). Throughout the nine months of gestation, Harriet is physically and emotionally tormented. As early as three months into the pregnancy, the child kicks violently from within the womb, a reminder, it seems to Harriet, that he is already in control, an early threat to her well-being. The fetus continues to grow at such a rapid pace that Harriet is terrified; its movements become so constant and painful that she unable to rest. She paces all night, cleans the house in the darkness, or indulges her now ravenous appetite for food—anything to quiet the beast within. Finally she resorts to tranquilizers, but even these only temporarily relieve her from an awareness of the baby's presence. Harriet comes to hate the child even before its birth.

Not surprisingly, Ben is a large baby at birth, resembling a "gnome, troll, or goblin" (49). The tremendous strength and potential violence he exhibited in the womb becomes more apparent when he enters the world. Harriet cannot breast feed him because he tears her breasts with his teeth in his effort to satisfy an insatiable appetite. Ben refuses any maternal attempts at cuddling or stroking, nor does he seem to recognize his parents at all. Instead of crying, he howls or roars in defiance. The other children quickly learn to stay out of his way after the cat and dog are both killed by his large, vice-like hands. David is the first to "disown" Ben, claiming that he is not human. Both Harriet and David feel that Ben "willed himself to be born" (58) and that he seems completely outside of their control. When Ben attempts to strangle his slightly older brother Paul, David suggests institutionalizing Ben. Harriet agrees for a time, but finally rescues Ben after finding him drugged and bound in a solitary chamber of the sanitarium. By returning Ben to the "fortress of peaceful domesticity," Harriet seems to have committed a treasonable act in the eyes of the other family members who had hoped to return to the bliss of pre-Ben living. Harriet attempts to make amends by keeping Ben in his own room, tranquilizing him, and, finally, allowing him to be "adopted" by street gangs with whom he seems to share some kind of bond. The novel ends with Ben, an adolescent, roaming the countryside with a band of lawless youths who rape, steal, and vandalize. Harriet and David are alone in their Victorian fortress, estranged from each other and their children who have left for other, less devastated environments.

From this summary it would be easy to dismiss Ben as another literary version of the "bad seed" motif, but he is much more. He embodies what Lessing sees as the end result of all our rationalizations about our own darker selves, the selves which continue to murder and destroy in ever more ingenious ways. He embodies the danger of denying (by drugging, institutionalizing, or imprisoning) what and who we are, and, most of all, he reminds us of how little control we have over our "representations" of reality. Ben represents the willful, tormented, unrestricted side of man, a side which David and Harriet have denied all of their lives. From the moment of his conception, he insists upon his place in the world and imposes his chaos on everyone and everything in his orbit. He cannot be contained or explained. Like Schopenhauer's will itself, Ben is both a product of the individual and of the world, the essence of both. What Harriet and David learn by the end of the novel is that Ben is their creation, literally and metaphysically. Literally, Ben mimics reality; he shows his family what they are *in essence*:

> When the children watched television, he squatted near them and looked from the screen to their faces, for he needed to know what reactions were appropriate. If they laughed, then, a moment later, he contributed a loud, hard, unnatural sounding laugh.... when they became silent and still with attention, because of some exciting moment, then he tensed his muscles, like them, and seemed absorbed in the screen—but really he kept his eyes on them. (69)

Like the will, Ben cannot be quieted permanently, not by drugs, imprisonment or activity. But again like the will, Ben is temporarily calmed by music. He will sit for hours and listen to musicals. Schopenhauer's theory on the power of music over the will is well known; this power has only a fleeting effect and the will, like Ben himself, must reassert itself. Ben's hunger for food and movement never ends, and he cannot be distracted by affection or matters of the intellect; he must simply keep moving, howling, roaring, feeding, destroying—to no end in particular. This, of course, is what puzzles Harriet most: why, she asks herself over and over again, why is this child the way he is? Is he a punishment for her previous happiness? Do she and David possess some inner darkness which came to the surface in this child (Harriet always believed that her sister's child was born with Down's Syndrome because of unhappiness in the marriage)? Her efforts to rationalize Ben are akin to man's constant desire to understand and satisfy the will, a desire which leads to more torment since such understanding and satisfaction are impossible. However, Harriet does come close to grasping the essence of Ben as pure will when she hypothesizes about the origin of "his kind."

> Harriet tries to establish a context for what has happened, mediating between a cosmic evolutionary perspective and an individual one. Her perception that the genes of "all those different people who lived on earth once—they must be in us somewhere" (*Fifth Child* 118) is counterbalanced by a sense that she and David are being punished for the hubris of wanting "to be better than anyone else" (*Fifth Child* 118), the victims of "punishing Gods, distributing punishments for subordination" (*Fifth Child* 118). Her final image of Ben, disappeared into the underworld of some metropolis where he searches for others of his kind, presents him as the harbinger of the future the Lovatts have tried to ignore. (Pickering 195)

In fact, Harriet finally reaches the conclusion that Ben is of a completely different origin than her other children, a genetic throwback to earlier man, a leftover from the underground civilizations: "It looked as if he believed he was hammering metal, forging something: one could easily imagine him, in the mines deep under the earth, with his kind" (70); "Ben makes you think . . . all those different people who lived on earth once—they must be in us somewhere—" (114); "Ben's people were at home under the earth, she was sure, deep underground in black caverns lit by torches. . . . Probably those peculiar eyes of his were adapted for quite different conditions of light" (122).

So while Harriet is unable to understand Ben and his direct significance to her (she continues to see him as something outside of herself rather than a manifestation of her own repressed will), she is able to see that he is not one single freakish aberration, that he is indeed a continuation of a previous essence, one that will continue on its irrational and frenzied course. As she reflects on the future of Ben and his companions at the end of the novel, Harriet muses ominously:

> And why should they stay in this country? They could easily take off and disappear into any number of the world's great cities, join

> the underworld there, live off their wits. Perhaps quite soon, in the new house she would be living in (alone) with David, she would be looking at the box, and there, in a shot on the News of Berlin, Madrid, Los Angeles, Buenos Aires, she would see Ben, standing rather apart from the crowd, staring at the camera with his goblin eyes, or searching the faces in the crowd for another of his kind. (132-133)

Clearly, there is a price to be paid for ignoring the "uglier" side of our nature, for attempting to suppress our baser instincts. Lessing always abhorred those who attempted to deny the darker side of reality, and Schopenhauer believed it impossible. That Ben will not only survive in the modern world, but truly thrive here, is unmistakable at the conclusion of *The Fifth Child*. His energy, the all-encompassing, endless striving of his being, pervades the world. Whether human beings will be able to channel this energy into something constructive or allow it to become the wind of destruction, Lessing and Schopenhauer leave as the question the future must answer.

Conclusion

This book is one of many recent studies of Schopenhauer's influence on nineteenth and twentieth century writers. His popularity as a visionary has grown in the last several decades, perhaps because of an interest in modernist and post-modernist pessimism, as well as urban naturalism and realism. Schopenhauer's philosophy has endured partly because it has adapted so well to the modern desire to understand, if not overcome, the horrors of existence, and partly because it helps to explain the endless parade of wars in this century and the continuing problems of poverty, starvation, and crime, problems we sometimes seem no closer to solving than in Schopenhauer's time. A philosophy which tries to explain these matters with cold objectivity, as cold and objective as the will itself, is a strange yet appealing comfort for modern day questors.

More than ever, women now participate in this quest. As the literature of Eliot, Schreiner, Woolf, and Lessing reveals, Schopenhauer speaks in an especially poignant way to the modern female in search of artistic and personal integrity. The answer Schopenhauer gives women is not in any sense positive or motivational on a humanist or feminist level. Yet it provides an explanation for the senseless spiritual and emotional annihilation women experience and for the endless wanting, striving, and suffering which form such a large part of women's fight for personhood, for the right to be a part of the very world which rejects their talents and intelligence. Schopenhauer argues that all mankind is unwelcome in the world, that the world itself is an objectification of the tormented will. Women find in this pessimistic environment some significant acceptance of their sense of alienation, and acceptance is no small comfort.

None of this explains or excuses Schopenhauer's misogyny, of course. But women writers cannot and do not dismiss Schopenhauer on this basis, just as they do not ignore the great ideas of so many misogynists, past and present. Women artists are most aware of hostility and rejection within the male world, and in order to overcome a desire to accept and surrender to their designated "place" far in the shadows of any given culture, they must discover the tools they need to survive and create hidden within the restrictive discourse of misogyny. Schopenhauer provides many of these literary, artistic, and psychological tools for women; his concept of the will forms a significant part of the female consciousness. For these reasons he can no longer be ignored in feminist studies.

Notes

Introduction

1. Remarkably, Schopenhauer never makes this connection, and nowhere in his works does he address the issue of women's particular susceptibility to the chains of the world. This he left to his literary daughters to illustrate.
2. One cannot resist wondering if Adele had possessed the same social mobility as her male counterpart, the freedom to travel alone, attend and teach at universities, write philosophy, would she have found, as Schopenhauer did, that life indeed offers some light to offset the shadows?
3. In 1819, Schopenhauer fathered a child—a daughter—but the child died only months after birth. No reaction or comment from Schopenhauer is available, only Adele's note of consolation, unanswered by Schopenhauer.
4. Schopenhauer always wanted to be revered by the British. There are probably several reasons for this. His father had wanted Arthur to be born in England, believing it to be a richer land of opportunity and culture than Germany. Schopenhauer grew up believing that Germans were rather dull and extremely resistant to new ideas, an opinion reinforced by his own country's persistent indifference to his life's work.

Chapter One, Part One

1. Josie Billington argues that it is Eliot's intention in *Middlemarch* to recast "the spirit of Christian values—love, pity, mercy, charity" into what she identifies as "Feuerbachian principles" of humanism (20). Eliot seems to recasting the notion of will with a similar, though Schopenhauerian, objective. Katherine Hughes attributes this need to look beyond conventional Christianity for both language and meaning to the death of Lewes's son and the unsatisfactory comfort offered by the standard church dogma (279).
2. As Knoepflmacher discusses, Caleb's words, in context, refer merely to Featherstone's last testament, but just as listeners in the novel hear a different, metaphysical meaning in his words (the lawyer replies, "That's a strange sentiment to come from a Christian man, by God!" [372]), the reader must hear a plea for all humanity in Caleb's simple wish as well.
3. Surely it is no coincidence that Casaubon's downfall is partly due to his ignorance of German. His dislike of anything German is evident when he is repulsed by the artist Naumann's German accent. His unwillingness to consider the fruits of German scholarship and his ability to read it are great flaws in Eliot's eyes. Will tells Dorothea that Casaubon's work is doomed to failure because it has long superseded by German scholars: "The Germans have taken the lead in historical inquiries, and they laugh at results which are got by groping about in the woods with a pocket-compass while they have made good roads" (240). Eliot herself was an avid admirer of German literature and philosophy, putting her in step with

nineteenth century enthusiasm for German life and literature. In addition to studying Schopenhauer, during the 1840's Eliot translated the German critic David Fredrich Strauss' *Das Leben Jesu* and Ludwig Feuerbach's *Das Wesen de Christentums*, and she was well-acquainted with the great works of German literature (Altick 221). Dorothea Barrett contends that "the school of German mythography to which Will refers had, by the time of the writing of *Middlemarch* (forty years after the time of its action), produced Friedrich Max Muller, who was personally acquainted with George Eliot" (140-41).

4. Barbara Hardy attributes Eliot's use of art to reflect morality solely to her interest in Arnold's *Culture and Anarchy*. But the language in *Middlemarch* throughout the passages cited indicates a thorough and serious understanding of Schopenhauer's aesthetics as well (Watt 310).

5. See W. J. Harvey's essay on Casaubon and Lydgate for other interesting similarities between these two men, including a discussion on the validity (or lack thereof) of their work.

6. See Keith Waddle's study of Mary Garth in which he argues for an interpretation of Mary as a "Wollstonecraftian feminist," based on her strong will, her intelligence, and her ability to survive through a renunciation of worldly seductions.

Chapter One, Part Two

1. For an insightful discussion of the Schopenhauerian role of music in *Daniel Deronda*, see McCobb's "The Morality of Musical Genius."

2. Though she does not discuss Schopenhauer, Delia da Sousa Correa addresses Eliot's interest in the Romantic school of music, particularly Mendelssohn, and the power Eliot gives music in the *Daniel Deronda*.

Chapter Two

1. For a complete discussion of the shortcomings of Zimmern's study, see my "Note on Browning and Schopenhauer," *Studies in Browning* 15 (1987): 51-54.

2. Schopenhauer explains: "Man attains to the state of voluntary renunciation, resignation, true composure, and complete willessness. At times, in the hard experience of our own sufferings or in the vividly recognized suffering of others, knowledge of the vanity and bitterness of life comes close to us. . . . We would like to deprive desires of their sting, close the entry to all suffering, purify and sanctify ourselves by complete and final resignation. But the illusion of the phenomenon soon ensnares us again; we cannot tear ourselves free. The allurements of hope, the flattery of the present, the sweetness of

pleasures, . . . all these draw us back to it, and rivet the bonds anew" (*WWR* I, 379).

3. Schreiner echoes most convincingly here Schopenhauer's contention that men are incapable of marital/sexual fidelity because of sound biological reasons, whereas fidelity on the part of women is natural (not a surprising or unique theory in the nineteenth century): "Man is inclined to inconstancy in love, woman to constancy. . . . The man can easily beget over a hundred children in a year . . . the woman . . . only one. . . . The man, therefore, always looks around for other women; the woman, on the contrary, cleaves firmly to the one man; for nature urges her, instinctively . . . to retain the nourisher and supporter [the father] of future offspring" (*WWR* II, 542). (See Introduction for Schopenhauer's later contradiction of this.) Schreiner, of course, uses this theory to point out the humanity of fidelity, the holy and spiritual affinity a woman feels for a man she loves, an awareness she suspects does not exist for the male. In a particularly poignant passage in *From Man to Man*, Rebekah attempts to make sense of her husband's need for extra-marital affairs, and she finally concludes, as Schopenhauer did, that men have innate need for conquest and possession unfamiliar to women who have never been led to believe they have a right—much less a need—to possess anything. Rebekah writes to her husband: "I don't think . . . I have ever wanted to catch anything that has tried to escape from me, an animal or a human creature. I have understood that what I wanted from living things was what they could give me, not what I could take from them. . . .What if for you a woman is only a "sport"? What if there is something in your nature which compels you to feel that the woman who has once wholly given herself to you is a dead bird, a fish, through whose gills you have put your fingers?" (269-70). Schopenhauer's answer would confirm Rebekah's hypothesis: "the man's love diminishes perceptibly from the moment it has obtained satisfaction" (*WWR* II, 542).

Chapter Three
1. In a 1995 article, David Alvarez discusses Schopenhauer's influence on George Moore's aesthetic philosophy and writing, specifically in *Esther Waters*.

2. See the studies of John de Gay and Nicholas Marsh for excellent discussions of form and content in Woolf's "word paintings."

Chapter Four, Part One
1. Lessing writes: "Readers like to think that a story [*Martha Quest*] is 'true'. 'Is it autobiographical?' is the demand. Partly it, as partly it is not. . . . If the novel is not the literal truth, then it is true in atmosphere, fully, more true than is this record, which is trying to be factual" (160-162). She goes on to discuss

how she obtained reading material of all kinds—philosophy, politics, sociology— from male friends, just as the Cohen boys furnished Martha Quest her little library. Oddly, Lessing never specifically mentions Schopenhauer in her list of books from her South Africa years, though he and Nietzsche figure prominently in Martha Quest's early education. One possible explanation for Lessing's omission in her autobiography comes from Josna Rege: Lessing "wishes to avoid any association with organized religion, along with all unquestioning systems of belief—ideologies, religious or secular—that trap people into habits of thought which blind them to the realities of the world around them" (123-124).

2. Muge Galin illustrates the limited kinship between Lessing's sufism and Schopenhauerian submission: "Lessing writes of Sufi truths and teaches *islam* or active submission to the higher will of Canopus or God while she also demands of her characters uncompromising independence and twentieth-century style rationalism and skepticism" (155). See also Shadia Fahim's 1994 study on Lessing's interest in sufism for a thorough treatment of its influence on her novels.

3. Lessing and Schopenhauer differ here only in semantics: as Hilde Laenan points out, "Schopenhauer holds onto the metaphysical concept 'soul', which he divides in 'will' on the one side, and 'intellect' on the other. Lessing speaks in psychological terms. She regards the psyche as the fusion of conscious—and unconsciousness" (311).

Bibliography

Aliotta, Antonio. *The Idealistic Reaction Against Science*. Trans. Agnes McCaskill. London: Macmillan, 1914.

Altick, Richard. *Victorian People and Ideas*. New York: Norton, 1973.

Alvarez, David. "The Case of the Split Self: George Moore's Debt to Schopenhauer in *Esther Waters*." *English Literature in Transition* 38 (1995): 169-185.

Argyros, Ellen. *"Without Any Check of Proud Reserve": Sympathy and Its Limits in George Eliot's Novels*. New York: Peter Lang, 1999.

Ashton, Rosemary. *George Eliot: A Life*. London: Penguin, 1996.

Barrett, Dorothea. *Vocation and Desire: George Eliot's Heroines*. London: Routledge, 1989.

Bell, Clive. *Art*. New York: Capricorn, 1958.

Berkman, Joyce Aurech. *Olive Schreiner: Feminism on the Frontier*. St. Albans, Vermont: Eden P, 1979.

Billington, Josie. "'What Can I Do?': George Eliot, Her Reader, and the Tasks of the Narrator in *Middlemarch*." *George Eliot–George Henry Lewes Studies* 31 (2000): 13-26.

Bodenheimer, Rosemarie. *The Real Life of Mary Ann Evans: George Eliot, Her Letters and Fiction*. Ithaca, New York: Cornell UP, 1994.

Bridgewater, Patrick. *George Moore and German Pessimism*. Durham: U of Durham, 1988: 11-57.

Cervetti, Nancy. "Mr. Dagley's Midnight Darkness: Uncovering the German Connection in George Eliot's Fiction." In *George Eliot and Europe*. Ed. John Rignall. Brookfield, Vermont: Ashgate, 1997: 84-97.

Clayton, Cherry. *Olive Schreiner*. New York: Twayne: 1997.

Correa, Delia da Sousa. "George Eliot and the Germanic 'Musical Magus'." In *George Eliot and Europe*. Ed. John Rignall. Brookfield, Vermont: Ashgate, 1997: 98-112.

Daiches, David. *A Critical History of English Literature*. Vol. II. New York: Ronald P, 1960.

Desmond, William. "Schopenhauer, Art, and the Dark Origin." In *Schopenhauer: New Essays in Honor of His 200th Birthday*. Ed. Eric von der Luft. Lewiston, New York: Mellen, 1988: 101-122.

Dibattista, Maria. *Virginia Woolf's Major Novels: The Fables of Anon*. New Haven and London: Yale UP, 1980.

Dowling, David. *Bloomsbury Aesthetics and the Novels of Forster and Woolf*. London: Macmillan, 1985.

Edel, Leon. *Bloomsbury: A House of Lions*. Philadelphia: Lippincott, 1979.

----------. *Henry James: The Untried Years*. Philadelphia: Lippincott, 1953.

Eliot, George. *Daniel Deronda*. New York: Penguin, 1986.

----------. *The Letters of George Eliot*. Ed. Gordon S. Haight. New Haven: Yale UP, 1955.

----------. *Middlemarch*. New York: Viking Penguin, 1965.

Fahim, Shadia S. *Doris Lessing: Sufi Equilibrium and the Form of the Novel*. New York: St. Martins, 1994.

Fry, Roger. *The Artist and Psychoanalysis*. London: Hogarth, 1924.

----------. *Cezanne*. New York: Noonday, 1960.

----------. *Vision and Design*. Harmondsworth: Pelican, 1937.

Galin, Muge. *Between East and West: Sufism in the Novels of Doris Lessing*. Albany, New York: State U of New York P, 1997.

Gay, John de. "Behind the Purple Triangle: Art and Iconography in *To the Lighthouse*." *Woolf Studies Annual* 5 (1999): 1-23.

Gilbert, Sandra M. And Susan Gubar. *The Madwoman in the Attic: The Woman Writer and the Nineteenth Century Literary Imagination.* New Haven: Yale UP, 1984.

Guth, Deborah. "George Eliot and Schiller: Narrative Ambivalence in *Middlemarch* and *Felix Holt.*" *Modern Language Review* 94 (1999): 913–924.

Hardy, Barbara. "*Middlemarch.*" In *The Victorian Novel.* Ed. Ian Watt. London: Oxford UP, 1971: 289-310.

Harvey, W. J. "*Middlemarch*: Casaubon and Lydgate." In *The Victorian Novel.* Ed. Ian Watt. London: Oxford UP, 1971: 311-323.

Hochberg, Shifra. "Animals in *Daniel Deronda*: Representation, Darwinian Discourse, and the Politics of Gender." *George Eliot–George Henry Lewes Studies* 30–31 (1996): 1–19.

Hughes, Kathryn. *George Eliot: The Last Victorian.* New York: Farrar, Strauss and Giroux, 1999.

Karl, Frederick R. *George Eliot: Voice of a Century.* New York: Norton, 1995.

Kertzer, J. M. "T.S. Eliot and the Problem of Will." *Modern Language Quarterly* 45 (Dec. 1984): 373-394.

Kim, Young–Moo. "Paradox of Sympathy: A Source of George Eliot's 'Romantic' Realism." *George Eliot–George Henry Lewes Studies* 32–33 (1997): 42–50.

Knoepflmacher, U.C. *Religious Humanism and the Victorian Novel.* Princeton: Princeton UP, 1965.

Laenan, Hilde. "The Metaphysics of Doris Lessing in Relation to the Philosophy of Arthur Schopenhauer." In *Just the Other Day: Essays on the Suture of the Future.* Ed. Luk DeVos. Vitgeverij EXA, Bouwhandelstraat 37, 2200 Antwerpen, 1985: 297-315.

Land, Stephen K. *Conrad and the Paradox of Plot.* London: Macmillan, 1984.

LeFew, Penelope A. "A Note on Browning and Schopenhauer." *Studies in Browning* 15 (1987): 51-54.

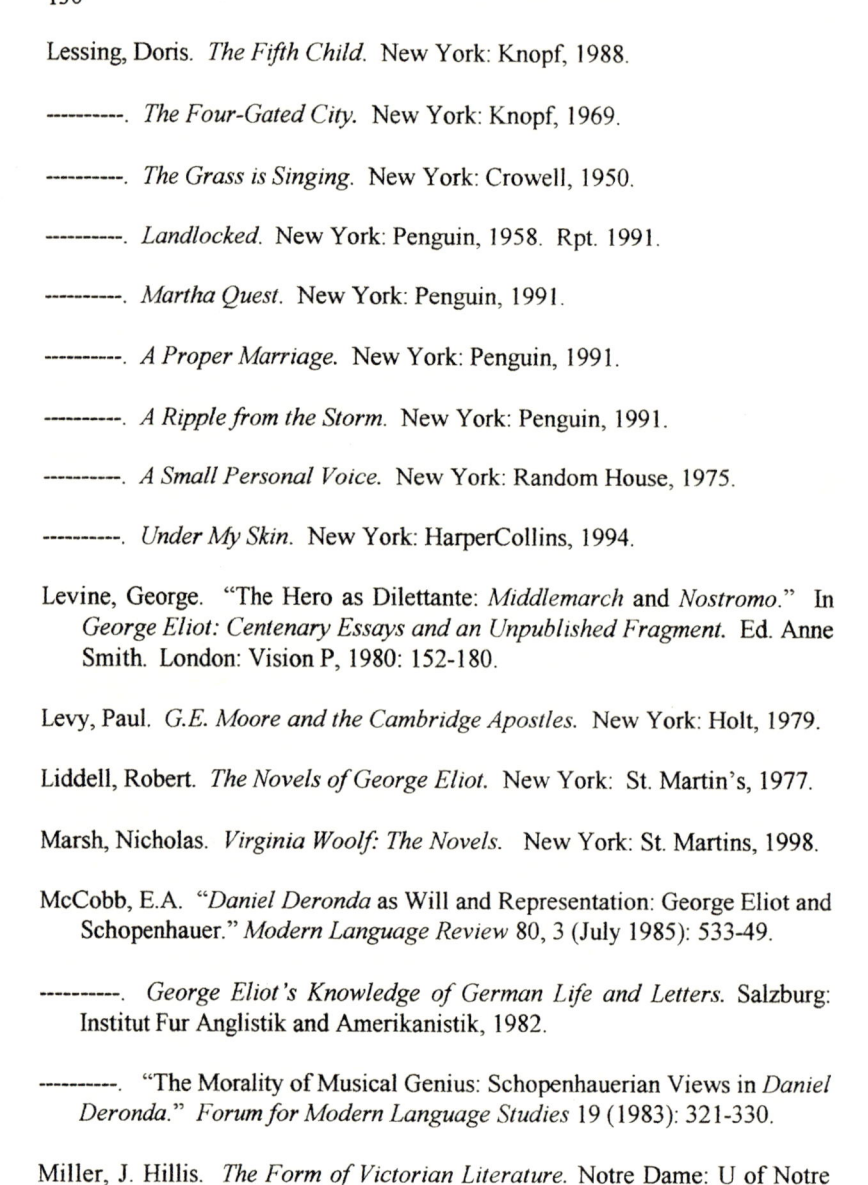

Lessing, Doris. *The Fifth Child.* New York: Knopf, 1988.

----------. *The Four-Gated City.* New York: Knopf, 1969.

----------. *The Grass is Singing.* New York: Crowell, 1950.

----------. *Landlocked.* New York: Penguin, 1958. Rpt. 1991.

----------. *Martha Quest.* New York: Penguin, 1991.

----------. *A Proper Marriage.* New York: Penguin, 1991.

----------. *A Ripple from the Storm.* New York: Penguin, 1991.

----------. *A Small Personal Voice.* New York: Random House, 1975.

----------. *Under My Skin.* New York: HarperCollins, 1994.

Levine, George. "The Hero as Dilettante: *Middlemarch* and *Nostromo*." In *George Eliot: Centenary Essays and an Unpublished Fragment.* Ed. Anne Smith. London: Vision P, 1980: 152-180.

Levy, Paul. *G.E. Moore and the Cambridge Apostles.* New York: Holt, 1979.

Liddell, Robert. *The Novels of George Eliot.* New York: St. Martin's, 1977.

Marsh, Nicholas. *Virginia Woolf: The Novels.* New York: St. Martins, 1998.

McCobb, E.A. "*Daniel Deronda* as Will and Representation: George Eliot and Schopenhauer." *Modern Language Review* 80, 3 (July 1985): 533-49.

----------. *George Eliot's Knowledge of German Life and Letters.* Salzburg: Institut Fur Anglistik and Amerikanistik, 1982.

----------. "The Morality of Musical Genius: Schopenhauerian Views in *Daniel Deronda*." *Forum for Modern Language Studies* 19 (1983): 321-330.

Miller, J. Hillis. *The Form of Victorian Literature.* Notre Dame: U of Notre Dame, 1968.

Minow–Pinkney, Makiko. "Reading Post–Modernism in *To the Lighthouse*." In *Virginia Woolf and Her Influences.* Eds. Laura Davis and Jeanette McVicher. New York: Pace UP, 1998.

Moore, G.E. *Philosophical Studies*. London: Routledge, 1965.

O'Donnell, Thomas J. "T.E. Lawrence and the Confessional Tradition: Either Angel or Beast." *Genre* 9 (1976): 135-151.

Oxenford, John. "Iconoclasm in German Literature." *Westminster Review* 9 (April 1853): 388-407.

Pickering, Jean. *Understanding Doris Lessing*. Columbia: U of South Carolina P, 1990.

Rege, Josna E. "Considering the Stars: The Expanding Universe of Doris Lessing's Work." In *Spiritual Exploration in the Works of Doris Lessing*. Ed. Phyllis Sternberg Perrakis. Westport, Connecticut: Greenwood, 1999: 121-134.

Reid, Panthea. *Art and Affection: A Life of Virginia Woolf*. New York: Oxford UP, 1996.

Rigney, Barbara Hill. "Hysteria and Sanity in *The Four-Gated City*." In *Doris Lessing: Modern Critical Views*. Ed. Harold Bloom. New York: Chelsea House, 1986: 133-49.

Robertson, Linda K. *The Power of Knowledge: George Eliot and Education*. New York: Peter Lang, 1997.

Rubenstein, Roberta. "*Briefing for a Descent into Hell*." In *Doris Lessing: Modern Critical Views*. Ed. Harold Bloom. New York: Chelsea House, 1986: 151-69.

----------. *The Novelistic Vision of Doris Lessing*. Urbana: U of Illinois P, 1979.

Safranski, Rudiger. *Schopenhauer and the Wild Years of Philosophy*. Cambridge: Harvard UP, 1990.

Schopenhauer, Arthur. *Essays and Aphorisms*. Trans. R. J. Hollingdale. Baltimore: Penguin, 1970.

----------. *The World as Will and Representation*. 2 Vols. Trans. E. F. J. Payne. New York: Dover, 1969.

Schreiner, Olive. *From Man to Man.* New York: Harper, 1927.

----------. *Letters of Olive Schreiner, 1876-1920.* Ed. S.C. Cronwright-Schreiner. London: T. Fisher Unwin, 1924. Rpt. 1976.

----------. *The Story of an African Farm.* Boston: Little, Brown, and Company, 1927.

Sukenick, Lynn. "Feeling and Reason in Doris Lessing's Fiction." In *Doris Lessing: Modern Critical Views.* Ed. Harold Bloom. New York: Chelsea House, 1986: 103-20.

Waddle, Keith A. "Mary Garth, The Wollstonecraftian Feminist of *Middlemarch*." *George Eliot–George Henry Lewes Studies* 28–29 (1995): 16-29.

Wallace, W. *Life and Writings of Arthur Schopenhauer.* London: Walter Scott Publishing, 1890.

Watt, Ian, ed. *The Victorian Novel.* London: Oxford UP, 1971.

Wiesenfarth, Joseph J. "Phillip Pirrip's Afterlife, or *Great Expectations* Again . . .and Again." *George Eliot–George Henry Lewes Studies* 36–37 (1999): 70-84.

Woolf, Virginia. *The Essays of Virginia Woolf, 1912-1918.* Vol. I. Ed. Andrew McNeillie. San Diego: Harcourt, 1987.

----------. *The Letters of Virginia Woolf.* 4 Vols. Eds. N. Nicholson and J. Trautmann. London: Hogarth, 1975-80.

----------. *To the Lighthouse.* San Diego: Harcourt Brace Jovanovich, 1989.

Zimmern, Helen. *Schopenhauer: His Life and Philosophy.* London: Allen, 1876. Rpt. 1932.

Index

Arnold, Matthew, 124(n)
Bell, Clive, 71ff
Conrad, Joseph, 11
Cronwright, S. C., 50, 61
Darwin, Charles, i, 9-10, 13, 16, 30
Eliot, George, 8, 9, 13-48
    Matthew Arnold and, 124(n)
    Charles Darwin and, 9-10, 13, 16, 30
    G.W. F. Hegel and, 9
    George Henry Lewes and, 13, 14, 35, 123(n)
    Schopenhauer and, 13-48
    Works,
        Daniel Deronda, 34-47, 54
        Middlemarch, 13-34, 36, 37,43, 123(n)
        Trans. of Strauss' *Das Leben Jesu*, 124(n)
        Trans. of Feuerbach's *Das Wesen de Christentums*, 124(n)
Eliot, T.S., 11
Ellis, Havelock, 49ff, 61
Emerson, Ralph Waldo, 60
Ford, Ford Madox, 11
Forster, E. M., 70
Fry, Roger, 70ff, 86
Gissing, George, 11
Goethe, Johann Wolfgang von, 3, 9,13, 17, 50
Hardy, Thomas, 11
Hegel, G. W. F., 9
Lawrence, D.H., 11
Lawrence, T.E., 11
Lessing, Doris, 3, 11, 126(n)
    Schopenhauer and, 89-114, 115-120
    Works,
        Children of Violence, series, 89-114
        The Fifth Child, 115-120
        The Four-Gated City, 109-114
        The Grass is Singing, 89-91
        Landlocked, 106-108
        Martha Quest, 91-95, 126(n)
        A Proper Marriage, 96-101
        A Ripple from the Storm, 101-106
        A Small Personal Voice, 90, 92, 94
Lewes, George Henry, 13, 14, 35, 123(n)
Meysenburg, Malwida von, 7
Moore, George, 70-72, 86, 125(n)
Ney, Elizabeth, 7
Oxenford, John, 8-12, 13
Pomeroy, Ernest Arthur George (Viscount Harberton), 69
Richter, Caroline, 5-6

Schopenhauer, Adele, 3-5, 123(n)
Schopenhauer, Arthur,
    Eliot's *Middlemarch* and, 13-34
    Fame and, 8-9
    Freud and, 94
    Lessing's *Children of Violence* and, 89-114, 126 (n)
        Lessing's *The Fifth Child* and, 115-120
    Misogyny and, 1-8, 123-124(n)
    Relationships, family, 3-6, 123(n)
    Relationships, women, 1-8 124(n)
    Schreiner's *From Man to Man* and, 59-68
    Schreiner's *Story of an African Farm* and, 49-59
    Views on music, 34ff, 124(n)
    Views on suicide, 44ff, 66ff, 124-125(n)
    Women writers and, 1-8, 121-122
    Woolf's *To the Lighthouse* and, 69-87
    Works,
        Essays and Aphorisms, 2, 52
        Parerga and Paralipomena, 1, 10
        The World as Will and Representation, 1, 7, 13-34, 35-48, 69-88, 89-114, 115-120 121, 122, 123(n), 124(n), 125(n)
Schopenhauer, Johanna, 3-4, 9
Schreiner, Olive, 6, 11, 15, 49-68, 89, 121, 124(n)
    S. C. Cronwright (husband) and, 50, 61
    Havelock Ellis and, 49, 61
    Ralph Waldo Emerson and, 60
    Doris Lessing and, 89
    Schopenhauer and, 49-68
    Herbert Spencer and, 60
    Works,
        From Man to Man, 59-68, 125(n)
        The Story of an African Farm, 49-59
        Women and Labour, 60
Shakespeare, William, 50, 63
Spenser, Herbert, 60

Virgil, *The Aeneid*, 85
Woolf, Leonard, 11, 70, 71
Woolf, Virginia, 69-88, 125(n)
    Clive Bell and, 71ff
    Roger Fry and, 70ff, 86
    E. M. Forster and, 70
    George Moore and, 70-72, 86, 125(n)
    Arthur Schopenhauer and, 1, 69-87
    Leonard Woolf and, 11, 70, 71
    Works,
    The Essays of, 69-70
    To the Lighthouse, 69-87
Wordsworth, William, 17, 95
Yeats, William Butler, 70
Zimmern, Helen,
    biography of Schopenhauer and, 49, 50, 124(n)

STUDIES IN COMPARATIVE LITERATURE

1. Ida H. Washington, **Echoes of Lucian in Goethe's** *Faust*
2. Jeanie Watson and Maureen Fries (eds.) **The Figure of Merlin in the Nineteenth and Twentieth Centuries**
3. B.R. Nelson, **The Basis of Morality and Its Relation to Dramatic Form in a Study of David Copperfield**
4. Nikki Stiller, **The Figure of Cressida in British and American Literature: Transformation of a Literary Type**
5. Maria Maddalena Colavito, **The Pythagorean Intertext in Ovid's** *Metamorphoses:* **A New Interpretation**
6. Thomas E. Connolly, **A Neo-Aristotelian and Joycean Theory of Poetic Forms**
7. Johan Callens, **From Middleton and Rowley's** *Changeling* **to Sam Shepard's** *Bodyguard*: **A Contemporary Appropriation of a Renaissance Drama**
8. John Parkin, **Henry Miller, The Modern Rabelais**
9. Sally MacEwen (ed.), **Views of Clytemnestra, Ancient and Modern**
10. Shirley M. Loui, **Murasaki's** *Genji* **and Proust's** *Recherche*: **A Comparative Study**
11. Lorne Shirinian, **Armenian-North American Literature: Genocide, Diaspora, and Symbols**
12. Alex Aronson, **Studies in Twentieth-Century Diaries: The Concealed Self**
13. Ella Whitehead (compiler), **John Lehmann's 'New Writing': An Author-Index 1936-1950**
14. Robert S. McCully, **The Enigma of Symbols in Fairy Tales: Zimmer's Dialogue Renewed**
15. Virginia M. Shaddy (ed.), **International Perspectives in Comparative Literature: Essays in Honor of Charles Dédéyan**
16. Shelly M. Quinn, **The Historical Development of Surrealism and the Relationships Between Hemispheric Specializations of the Brain**
17. Jean Andrews, **Spanish Reactions to the Anglo-Irish Literary Revival in the Twentieth Century: The Stone By the Elixir**
18. Yoseph Milman, **Opacity in the Writings of Robbe-Grillet, Pinter, and Zach: A Study in the Poetics of Absurd Literature**
19. David Blamires, ***Fortunatus* in His Many English Guises**
20. M.L. Harvey, **Iambic Pentameter From Shakespeare to Browning: A Study of Generative Metrics**
21. Michael E. Moriarty, **Semiotics of World Literature**

22. Tan Ye, **Common Dramatic Codes in Yüan and Elizabethan Theaters: Characterization in *Western Chamber* and *Romeo and Juliet***
23. Terry J. Martin, **Rhetorical Deception in the Short Fiction of Hawthorne, Poe, and Melville**
24. Terry John Converse, **The Psychology of the Grotesque in August Strindberg's** *The Ghost Sonata*
25. Thomas E. Connolly, **Essays on Fiction–Dickens, Melville, Hawthorne, and Faulkner**
26. Aixue Wang, **A Comparison of the Dramatic Work of Cao Yu and J.M. Synge**
27. William S. Haney II and Nicholas O. Pagan (eds.), **The Changing Face of English Literary and Cultural Studies in a Transnational Environment**
28. Cynthia Whitney Hallett, **Minimalism and the Short Story–Raymond Carver, Amy Hempel. and Mary Robison**
29. Charles A. Carpenter, **Dramas of the Nuclear Age-A Descriptive List of English-Language Plays**
30. Hiroko Harada, **Aspects of Post-War German and Japanese Drama (1945-1970): Reflections on War, Guild, and Responsibility**
31. Morton D. Rich, **The Dynamics of Tonal Shift in the Sonnet**
32. James Maurice Ivory, **Identity and Narrative Metamorphoses in Twentieth-Century British Literature**
33. Kathleen R. Johnson, **Understanding Children's Animal Stories**
34. Margaret Jubb, **The Legend of Saladin in Western Literature and Historiography**
35. Dennis Quinn, **Edmund Spenser's *Faerie Queene* and the Monomyth of Joseph Campbell: Essays in Interpretation**
36. Jaquelyn W. Walsh, **The Impact of Restoration Critical Theory on the Adaptation of Four Shakespearean Comedies**
37. Megan Gribskov Painter, **The Aesthetic of the Victorian Dramatic Monologue**
38. Patrick R. Burger, **The Political Unconscious of the Fantasy Sub-Genre of Romance**
39. Andrew Ginger, John Hobbs and Huw Lewis (eds.), **Selected Interdisciplinary Essays on the Representation of the Don Juan Archetype in Myth and Culture**
40. Kelly Younger, **Irish Adaptations of Greek Tragedies: Dionysus in Ireland**
41. Roger Whitehouse (ed.), **Literary Expressions of Exile: A Collection of Essays**
42. Penelope LeFew-Blake, **Schopenhauer, Women's Literature, and the Legacy of Pessimism in the Novels of George Eliot, Olive Schreiner, Virginia Woolf, and Doris Lessing**